CHATHAM HOUSE ESSAYS: 4

STERLING IN THE SIXTIES

CHATHAM HOUSE ESSAYS

It is proposed to publish under this general title short studies designed to illuminate and to provoke discussion of issues in the field of international affairs. Previous essays in the series have been:

1   *The Chinese View of Their Place in the World.* By C. P. FITZGERALD

2   *The China-India Border: The Origins of the Disputed Boundaries.* By ALASTAIR LAMB

3   *The Debatable Alliance: An Essay in Anglo-American Relations.* By CORAL BELL

Sterling in the Sixties

BY

CHRISTOPHER McMAHON

Issued under the auspices of the
Royal Institute of International Affairs

OXFORD UNIVERSITY PRESS

LONDON   NEW YORK   TORONTO

1964

Oxford University Press, Amen House, London E.C.4

GLASGOW NEW YORK TORONTO MELBOURNE WELLINGTON
BOMBAY CALCUTTA MADRAS KARACHI LAHORE DACCA
CAPE TOWN SALISBURY NAIROBI IBADAN ACCRA
KUALA LUMPUR HONG KONG

Printed in Great Britain by
The Bowering Press, Plymouth

Contents

v

I

Introduction

OCCASIONALLY the world gratifies the tidy-minded by clustering important and related events close together in time. Anyone interested in international monetary arrangements in general, and sterling in particular, is likely, for example, to find 1947–8 a key date. The spectacularly unsuccessful convertibility of sterling, the Marshall Aid legislation, and the setting up of OEEC brought about and embodied at that time a major change in American and European attitudes. A decade later, in 1958, another fundamental change in both the real payments situation and attitudes towards it was symbolized by the birth of EEC, the death of EPU, the convertibility of the main European currencies, and the appearance of a large deficit on the U.S. balance of payments.

It is notoriously difficult to tell at the time whether one is on a watershed. But 1963–4 may well prove to have been a third significant date. In the five years from 1958 to 1963 there was a rising volume of discussion, argument, and negotiation on four interrelated subjects: Britain's entry into the Common Market; the limitations imposed on Britain's growth by her balance of payments; the persistence of the U.S. deficit; and the adequacy or otherwise of international liquidity. It may well be that Britain's failure to gain membership of the Common Market will help bring the other matters to a head. In any case 1963 was characterized by a much more urgent attitude towards the U.S. balance of payments and by some unprecedented steps by the U.S. authorities. There is evidence of changes in thinking on the U.K. balance of payments too; and these developments combined may have important consequences for world liquidity arrangements. As this is written, it is too early to say whether there will be a change in government in the U.K.; or whether the change in the Managing Directorship of the IMF will have significant effects. But in any case it seems a good moment for a brief review of sterling's position in the world.

Any such review will be greatly coloured by the writer's expectations about the U.K. balance of payments. It seems right, therefore, to state one's views on this subject at the outset. Briefly, my expectation is that the U.K. balance of payments will be a good deal healthier over the next, say, five years or so than at any time since the war. But this is not based on a lot of detailed forecasts of trade trends. In so far as it is not purely hunch it is based on such considerations as the following.

First, the EEC countries appear to be running into problems of cost-inflation very similar to those this country has long been plagued with. Already there has been considerable improvement in the U.K.'s cost position relative to the Continental countries; and this may go further. I believe that the only way of tackling cost inflation is by way of an incomes policy; and the U.K. is probably nearer to achieving a workable incomes policy (despite the enormous difficulties) than any of her main competitors. Secondly, I think the source of much of the U.K.'s trouble over the past decade can be summed up as 'too little room to manoeuvre'. In the future there is likely to be more room to manoeuvre, as the economy is managed more flexibly and gets more help from outside. (This point is discussed in later chapters.) Thirdly, despite the frequent deflationary pronouncements of many of the Continental central bankers and monetary authorities, and the recent sluggishness of the U.S. economy, I am inclined to bet on a reasonably brisk expansion of activity in the industrialized countries over the next few years. The Common Market is, in a sense, committed to expansion; and if the Commission has its way—rather a big 'if' admittedly—the development of co-ordinated indicative planning may make a contribution towards maintaining a fast rate of growth. The U.S. economy is showing signs of expansion at last and the tax cuts should give further stimulus. The programme for co-ordinated expansion within OECD and the development of international monetary co-operation may also be helpful.

Fourthly, as far as the U.K. herself is concerned, it seems likely to me that her technological backwardness (and general hopelessness) has been oversold. As Samuel Brittain pointed out in a stimulating article recently[1] (though he was talking about an incomes policy) when *everybody* is agreed on something it is probably no longer the case. I think large and fundamental changes in ways of thinking and doing things have been taking place in this country in recent years—developments in the building industry and the civil service might provide two important instances—and that these are likely soon to show tangible results.

However, it would be the simplest thing in the world to knock down all the above suggestions and show that everything was still for the worst. Moreover, even if one can bolster one's optimism with a great deal of detailed statistical material, one should remain cautious. Always a hazardous operation, forecasting is a more than usually thankless business in the case of the balance of payments.

To all the normal difficulties some particularly intractable ones are added. There are more variables involved, and their interrelations are more complicated and obscure, than in say the level of activity of a single country. More-

[1] In *The Twentieth Century*, Summer 1963.

over, what is being forecast is a small percentage difference between two large magnitudes:[2] total external payments and receipts are for the U.K. each of the order of £7,000 million, while the current balance fluctuates between outside limits of plus and minus £300 million. Thus even if we are forecasting only one year ahead we can predict an overall balance instead of a rather serious deficit, simply by forecasting receipts 1 per cent too high and payments 1 per cent too low. Projecting the balance for several years or trying to estimate an average level over a period of some time can produce through a cumulation of tiny errors a wildly wrong picture.

There is also a problem of a rather different kind. With some economic magnitudes—for example the rate of growth of national output—a number of different forecasts based on different assumptions could all be potentially correct. It is perfectly possible that on certain assumptions the economy might grow at a fairly steady rate of 2 per cent per annum indefinitely, while on other assumptions (or policies) a growth rate of 4 per cent might be sustained. But in the case of the balance of payments (for the U.K. at any rate) it is impossible for a deficit of more than a certain size to persist for any length of time. Something will have to be done about it. Thus forecasting a balance of payments is inextricably mixed up with forecasting the ways in which surpluses or deficits are financed and the measures which are taken to correct disequilibria as they arise.

It is disheartening, when looking at forecasts of all kinds of variables, to find how large a proportion of them is made up of simple extrapolation; or, perhaps more often, of extrapolation with cold feet—i.e. counting on something

[2] Which are, however, themselves small in relation to aggregate demand or supply. As Sir Donald MacDougall has put it, one is trying to forecast 'a marginal part of a marginal part' (*The Dollar Problem: a Reappraisal* (Princeton, 1961)).

to continue to rise or fall as it has been doing, only not quite as fast. In some areas there may be great virtues in this approach. I understand, for example, that one can equal or improve on any meteorological office's perform-ance over a long run simply by forecasting for each day: 'the same as yesterday'; whether such a forecast *really is* a forecast is perhaps a question for the philosophers.

In economics, however, and especially international economics, the dangers of being misled on a grand scale by extrapolation have surely been underlined in the past decade. In the immediate post-Korean period, for example, it was widely expected that the terms of trade would continue as a long-term trend to move against the industrialized countries—though not as fast as they had recently been doing; ever since, of course, they have been moving in the opposite direction. The way the dollar gap turned into a dollar surplus provides an even more striking and well-documented example. And it is easy to forget how pessimistic everybody was about the French economy only five or six years ago—and about the German economy five or six years before that. Perhaps the deep malaise we now all find so readily in the U.K.[3] will look similarly odd in five years time. Who knows? The U.S. balance of pay-ments may be in surplus before then.

Things do in fact change much faster than we expect. One of the reasons for this, at least in the field of the balance of payments, may be that there are many cumula-tive effects. Whereas at one time it appeared normal for a deficit in a country's current account to be accompanied by an inflow on capital account, nowadays current and capital accounts often appear to be strong or weak to-gether. A weak current account may be associated with a weak competitive-cost position so that there is inducement for investment capital to go elsewhere; and where there is

[3] See *Encounter*, July 1963, and the latest list of any serious publisher.

weakness on current and long-term capital account combined, there are likely to be outflows of short-term capital
because of speculation against the exchange rate. In such
a situation a relatively small fundamental improvement
may quite radically change the entire situation.[4]

There is also the fact that, the world being what it is,
innumerable things are wrong, or less than perfect, in an
economy at any time. When things are bad, it is easy to
invoke in aid of an explanation of the general weakness,
any or all of a myriad of individual shortcomings. Then,
since it will seem unlikely that these can all be soon put
right, there will be a strong tendency to believe that the
weakness will continue for a long time. In fact, however, a
change in relatively few variables or conditions may be
enough to do the trick. Suppose that the statistics told us
that the French economy and balance of payments were
now in a very poor state: just think of all the plausible
explanations we could provide for this.

Enough has been said to explain why although my basic
assumption is that the U.K. balance of payments is likely
to be better in the future than it has been in the recent past,
I am not optimistic enough to believe that there will be *no*
problem (in the sense in which one can say that the EEC
countries have had no balance-of-payments problems in
the last few years). Corrective measures will doubtless have
to be taken from time to time; but perhaps not as urgently
or often as has been the case.

Briefly, the plan of the rest of the book is as follows.
Section 2 discusses the nature of the U.K. balance-of-
payments 'problem' and the ways in which this may be
masked or brought out by the presentation of the accounts.
Section 3 is concerned with the kinds of measures which

---

[4] See J. Downie, *What can the United States learn from foreign experience?*
(paper delivered to a conference on Unemployment and the American
Economy at Berkeley, California, April 1963).

have been and might be adopted to manage the balance of payments; it is suggested that there is often confusion over what particular measures could or are intended to do. Section 4 and 5 deal in rather more detail with two major balance-of-payments adjustment policies: deflation and devaluation. In Section 6 international capital movements, capital markets, and capital controls are taken up; the situations for the major currencies are reviewed and the possible functions of sterling discussed. Then in Section 7 the role of sterling as a reserve currency is reached: what is and should be its relation to the dollar, to the European currencies and to the IMF? Finally, Section 8 offers a short conclusion and some general thoughts on the way things might develop.

2

The Criterion of Success in Managing the Balance of Payments

The identification of the problem

No speech by an economic statesman nowadays is complete without a reference to the four aims of a modern government's economic policies—growth, full employment, price stability, and a sound balance of payments—and the difficulties of achieving all four at once. But there is insufficient emphasis given to the relationship these aims bear to one another. Growth is clearly an end—in so far as there is such a thing as an economic end. We don't want economic growth for any other economic reason: we simply want it. Most people would regard full employment as an end too—though there is disagreement on how far it should be pressed if it is in conflict with growth. Most people would regard price stability as desirable primarily in so far as it proved a means to the attainment of the other goals—though some people (especially in the U.S.) seem to regard it as an end in itself to achieve which it is reasonable to accept a lower growth rate and lower employment. The balance of payments, however, cannot properly be regarded as an end. It is often a crucial constraint: only if the balance of payments is right (in some sense) is there any prospect of *future* growth or full employment; but it does not make sense to prefer a better balance of payments to say faster growth, *in the long run*.[1]

[1] To classify economic objectives as 'ends' and 'means' (as is done here) is crude and arbitrary and may be misleading. To see how arbitrary and misleading, consult P. P. Streeten, 'Programmes and Prognoses', *Quarterly Journal of Economics*, August 1954. But a basic distinction between the balance of payments and growth remains.

This is an obvious enough point when it is stated, but it is often missed in practice. Thinking about the balance of payments is likely to be muddled unless it is borne in mind.

What is the nature of the constraint exercised by the balance of payments? What is the criterion of success in managing it? The plain man's immediate answer is likely to be something along the lines: 'We must pay our way' or, more precisely, 'We must earn enough from our exports to pay for our imports.' This was indeed the criterion put forward by government spokesmen in the early post-war years; and on this criterion the U.K. has been quite successful. In the thirteen years from 1950 to 1962 there were deficits on current account in only four years, and there was an average surplus of £70 million.

There are two reasons why this performance cannot be taken to represent success. The first is that because of the smallness of the U.K. reserves she simply could not have *allowed* a deficit in her current account to continue for any length of time. She *had* to keep it at least in balance; and therefore to see how sound her balance-of-payments position was one must look, not simply at the balance-of-payments figures themselves, but at how they came about —at the cost to the economy of the current surplus that was achieved. Many people would hold, as I should myself, that there was a heavy cost in terms of slower growth than would otherwise have been possible.

The second reason why achieving a balance on current account is an inadequate criterion for a successful balance of payments is strikingly illustrated by the U.S., which has averaged a 'current' *surplus* (U.K. definition) of $2¾ billion (i.e. thousand million) each year for the past five years when we have heard so much about the U.S. 'deficit', and when there was an outflow of gold from the U.S. averaging $1.4 billion a year.

The balance-of-payments accounts of any country must algebraically add to zero. But they can be arbitrarily re-arranged and divided at an infinite number of points so that the items above the line may be added to give a 'surplus' or 'deficit' while the items below the line are taken to show how the 'surplus' or 'deficit' was financed. Where one draws the line will depend on one's interests and preconceptions; on political and economic value judgements about the economy as a whole and its place in the world.

During the 1950s in the U.K. the 'line' was implicitly shifted farther down the accounts. The government spoke of the need not merely to be in balance on current account but to earn a surplus to enable us to lend and invest abroad and to build up our reserves. The size of the current-account surplus to be aimed at—to be considered as par—was gradually raised from £200 million to £450 million, though unfortunately the surplus actually achieved tended gradually to fall. Similarly the massive U.S. surpluses on current account have been more than offset in recent years by outflows for foreign aid and private investment. Over the same period the presentation of the U.K. balance-of-payments accounts was simplified and re-organized till it assumed its present form in which it is relatively easy to see how far the newer aims are being achieved. The accounts are divided into three parts—current account, long-term capital account, and monetary movements. The first contains exports and imports of goods and services (including government expenditure abroad on defence and grants to underdeveloped countries). The second contains all movements, both inward and outward, of long-term capital: direct investment, portfolio investment, and long-term loans, both government and private. The third account contains movements of the reserves, of short-term claims on foreigners ('miscellaneous capital'), and short-term liabilities to foreigners ('sterling balances').

From this presentation it is easy to get an arithmetical answer to the question 'How much of any year's current surplus was used up by overseas investment?' This calculation is in fact often done and the conclusion often drawn that we should act to reduce our long-term capital outflow so that our hard-won current surplus can directly add to our inadequate reserves. This pseudo-causal way of looking at the accounts is of course most misleading. There is no reason to suppose that the current surplus is in some sense amassed first, and then 'spent' on aid or acquiring long-term assets overseas. In principle (and quite often in practice) it may be the other way round: exports may be generated by the outflow of capital. This is not to deny that there may be a case for restricting investment abroad. A reduction of capital outflow by £x million would normally reduce the current surplus by less than £x million, and hence imply some benefit to the monetary account. Most of those who urge reduction of long-term investment or overseas military expenditure or aid in the interests of strengthening the balance of payments are well aware that the net benefits of their proposals to the reserves are likely to be less than the gross benefits. But the temptation to match one part of the accounts against another as specifically causing or offsetting it is very strong; to classify the accounts at all is to succumb to this temptation in some measure. We cannot remind ourselves too often that the accounts are a seamless web.

One is also encouraged by the present U.K. classification to think of the current and long-term capital balances combined as comprising an 'overall' or *'fundamental'* surplus or deficit which is 'financed' by the monetary movements. The distinction between 'autonomous' and 'compensating' or 'financing' changes has been much discussed in the theoretical literature on the balance of payments. The distinction is an important and helpful one in principle and one might say that one of the purposes of a good set of balance-of-payments accounts is to enable the reader to make it. But it may be asked whether the present U.K. classification makes the right distinction, focuses our attention on the right problem. Should we be worried as long as we are not running a surplus on current and long-term capital combined, and content if we are?

I should like to answer to both halves of this question 'Not always'. Useful and sensible though the present U.K. classification is in many ways, I think it is misleading in others, and has helped to foster some unsatisfactory attitudes and policies toward the U.K. balance of payments. I should like to suggest an alternative way of presenting the accounts which puts the emphasis rather differently.

Alternative classifications of the accounts

There has been a lot of interest in the U.S. in the past couple of years in the presentation of the U.S. balance-of-payments accounts. This is primarily because the official U.S. statisticians have 'drawn the line' at a rather unusual place with the result that the official figure for the deficit (which we have heard so much about in recent years) is normally considerably larger than it would be if the U.S. accounts were classified in the same way as those for the U.K.[2] Suggestions for an alternative presentation have

[2] The most important difference between the official U.K. and U.S. accounts is that in the U.K. accounts flows of both domestic and foreign short-term capital are included 'below the line' under monetary movements (as 'sterling liabilities' and miscellaneous capital), while in the U.S. accounts movements of foreign short-term capital are put below the line but movements of domestic short-term capital are not. They appear 'above the line' together with domestic and foreign capital movements. The attacks on this asymmetry by Lary and others (see below) seem unanswerable.

been made by a number of people.[3] I am going to devote a little time to one of these studies because the arguments raised in it have a good deal of relevance to the U.K. position.[4] Mr Lary would like to see the U.S. accounts presented in the same basic way as those for the U.K. are, and the reasons he advances constitute a good explanation and defence of the official U.K. approach.

His first reason is that what we can call 'the U.K. approach' draws 'the line' nearer to the conceptually ideal division between autonomous and compensating movements. He admits, as of course the official U.K. statisticians would admit, that some of the monetary movements may not simply passively reflect movements in the other two accounts but may actually engender them. An extension of trade credit that makes possible an increase in exports is an example. But no division will ever be conceptually perfect, and it is probably true that most changes in the current and long-term capital account could be regarded as autonomous and most changes in the monetary account as compensating.

A second criterion of success or failure in managing the balance of payments, which can be used to justify drawing the line where the U.K. accounts draw it, is the improve-

(Although see the article by Walther Lederer in Seymour Harris, ed., *The Dollar in Crisis* (N.Y., 1961), for a defence of the official practice.) The practical consequences of the classification is that in years (such as 1960 and 1961) when there is a large outflow of short-term capital, the official figure for the U.S. deficit is substantially larger than it would be on the basis of the U.K. accounts. See Table I, p. 22.

[3] During 1963 President Kennedy set up a Committee on Balance of Payments Statistics to report on the most satisfactory classification. The study by the Brookings Institute, *The U.S. Balance of Payments in 1968* (which I did not see until this chapter was in draft), puts forward a classification basically similar to that of the U.K.

[4] Hal B. Lary, *Problems of the United States as World Trader and Banker.* (N.Y., National Bureau of Economic Research, 1963), espec. pp. 137–60. Although, as its title suggests, this book is primarily concerned with the U.S. balance of payments, it contains some general discussion of the nature of balance-of-payments problems, the concepts of surplus and deficit, &c, to which the present writer is indebted, and the interested reader is directed.

ment or deterioration in the country's external liquidity position. All the elements in the monetary account—gold and currency reserves, sterling liabilities, and miscellaneous short-term capital—are by definition short-term or liquid liabilities and claims; and a change in this account might therefore be taken to represent an improvement or a deterioration in liquidity; a decrease or an increase in the vulnerability of the reserves, or indeed of the exchange rate. Alternatively one might wish to take as one's indicator only the reserves and the sterling liabilities; this is in effect what the official statistics do for the U.S. and this is the principal reason (i.e. to indicate changes in liquidity or vulnerability) why they do it.[5]

But neither collection of monetary movements is in fact very helpful for this purpose. As has often been pointed out, many assets which are short-term in form may be rolled over and over, and thus be effectively long-term in reality; for example, Treasury bills or short-term government stock held by Commonwealth governments; or some proportion of many private current bank accounts. Again, many so-called long-term claims and liabilities— e.g. equity investment—may in practice be highly liquid. A slightly different point, equally important, is that when the ratio between reserves and (so called) liquid liabilities outstanding is of the order of $1 : 3\frac{1}{2}$, as it is for the U.K., marginal variations in either the assets or the liabilities cannot have much influence on the potential vulnerability of sterling. Of course, tiny changes in a number of variables can in practice influence the strength of sterling: but the point is that the influence of such changes could not be gauged simply by looking at the numerical changes in the elements in the monetary balance. In any case, as is pointed out below (p. 27), a given improvement or deterioration in the monetary account will have different

[5] See the article by Walther Lederer quoted in note 2 above.

significance according as it results from a change in reserves or a change in liabilities.

Finally, Lary suggests a third reason for drawing the 'line' where the U.K. accounts draw it. He claims that all the items in the monetary account are alike in being 'sensitive to monetary policy'. He defines 'monetary policy' for this purpose rather widely, appearing to include any kind of intervention by the monetary authorities in the markets for liquid funds. What he is emphasizing as the common quality of the items below the 'line' is their 'sensitivity'. These are the items, he says, where the authorities can produce relatively quick, large, and certain effects, whereas the items above the line are influenced chiefly by general economic forces or political or military decisions.

The kind of distinction Lary wishes to make (i.e a distinction in terms of how the authorities can affect the situation) seems to me right but I am not convinced that his particular distinction can be used to justify the U.K. division of the accounts. For a country with exchange control over long-range capital movements, Lary's distinction would not seem to coincide with the distinction between monetary account on the one hand, and the current and long-term capital accounts on the other. Indeed, since he wrote, the new interest-equalizing tax proposed by the U.S. authorities may be going to bring much of the longer-term capital account below Lary's 'line' even for the U.S.

So much for the case for the 'overall' or 'basic' balance of payments. What may be said against it?

A 'market balance'

Briefly, I think that it makes too sharp a distinction between so-called 'basic', 'real', 'underlying' elements in the balance on the one hand, and the so-called 'volatile', 'temporary' elements on the other. There are several reasons why such a distinction may be misleading.

The first of these may be stigmatized as a purely technical one: it is the striking growth and current average size of the 'balancing item'.[6] In five of the last eight years the balancing item has been of the same order as, or larger than, the current and long-term capital balance. In these circumstances it becomes impossible to describe what has been happening in such terms as 'there was a current surplus of x but a net capital outflow of y so that there was an improvement of x-y in our monetary position'. What we have to say is 'there was a current surplus of x and a net capital outflow of y and an improvement (or a deterioration) of z in our monetary position', where x, y, and z are unrelated. *Ex hypothesi* we do not know what makes up the balancing item. It is probably largely unrecorded short-term capital movements but there are always likely to be elements from the long-term capital balance and even from the current balance.[7] Thus it probably does not fall entirely on one side of the 'line' or the other.

However, quite apart from the egregious balancing item, several developments in the international payments system in recent years have conspired to make the official classification less helpful. First, there has been a striking increase in international flows of private capital of all kinds—long and short. There are many reasons for this: the relaxation of exchange controls in the U.K. and Con-

[6] This is, of course, what other countries call 'errors and omissions'. Perhaps there is a case for the U.K. adopting this nomenclature too. 'Errors and omissions' may carry unwarranted overtones of carelessness, but it does not suggest, as surely 'balancing item' does, that the statisticians are in control of the situation; and it underlines the fact that this is not really an item at all, merely a reminder that other items are wrong.

[7] See *Bank of England Quarterly Bulletin*, Mar. 1962 and *National Institute Economic Review*, Feb. 1962 for articles on the composition of the balancing item.

tinental countries; the attractions of the developing Common Market for American and British capital; the disequilibrium in international payments with the consequent recurrent suspicions of the pound and the dollar; the desire of the Governor of the Bank of England to revive London as an international financial centre, &c. Whatever the reasons, private capital has been moving more and in more different forms than for many years. On the other hand there has been an equally striking growth in international monetary co-operation, both multilateral and bilateral. The IMF has been much more used; and individual monetary authorities have shown themselves willing to increase their holdings of sterling or dollars, for a time at least, to help defend the two currencies when they are under attack (e.g. the so-called Basle arrangements of 1961 and 1963 for sterling, and the currency 'swaps' negotiated by the Americans (pp. 95–97 below).

Taken together, these developments have meant that stressing the difference between long-term and short-term capital may be less useful (at least for some purposes) than distinguishing between on the one hand all flows undertaken for private reasons, or for any reasons other than protecting the exchange rate, and on the other hand official compensatory or financing measures. Such a distinction is, of course, not new in balance-of-payments literature. But it has recently been given some prominence by Messrs Walter Gardner and Robert Triffin who have suggested that the U.S. balance-of-payments accounts be reclassified in this way.[8] There would be much to com-

---

[8] See Walter Gardner, 'An Exchange-Market Analysis of the U.S. Balance of Payments', *IMF Staff Papers*, May 1961; and Robert Triffin, 'The Presentation of U.S. Balance of Payments Statistics; General Comments', in American Statistical Association, *1961 Proceedings of the Business and Economics Statistics Section* (Washington, 1962). Lary (pp. 155–60) discusses the Gardner and Triffin proposals (which are very similar) but, as we have seen, prefers a classification more like the present U.K. one.

mend its adoption—at least as an alternative to the present classification—for the U.K. Table 2 (p. 24) sets out the U.K. balance-of-payments accounts for the years 1958–62 on both the official basis and a 'market-balance'[9] basis. Before discussing the point of the reclassification, we should briefly discuss the placing of the various items. Broadly, all private transactions go into the market balance and all official transactions into compensatory movements; but there are exceptions to this. Current government transactions are put in the market balance on the grounds that though balance-of-payments considerations are obviously relevant to the size of such items as overseas defence expenditure, grants to colonies, expenditure on the diplomatic service, &c, they are not so important in influencing the magnitudes as between one year and another. Decisions on these matters, though taken directly by the government, are different in kind from, say, a decision whether to borrow from the IMF. A more difficult question is posed by intergovernmental long-term loans. Some of these—e.g. aid loans to underdeveloped countries—are obviously very like much of current government expenditure overseas and should therefore be included with it in the market balance. We should have a category called 'foreign aid' or 'development aid' in the accounts as the Americans do. On the other hand many of the other items in 'government long-term capital' are obviously 'compensatory' in nature; e.g. the loan by the U.S. Export-Import Bank to the U.K. at the time of the sterling crisis in 1957 and its repayment in 1959; or the advance repayments of debt to the U.K. by Western Europe. Even the yearly repayments of the U.S. post-war loan may be skipped in an emergency. Moreover, since 1957 the movements of 'government long-term

---

[9] The term 'market balance' derives from Gardner, but the particular arrangement of the accounts suggested here differs somewhat from his.

capital', apart from development aid, have been dominated by 'compensatory' flows. Hence we put these below the line.

The logic of the market balance demands that while *official* sterling holdings be put below the line, unofficial or private sterling holdings go above it. This is certainly not entirely satisfactory. The division of a country's holdings of sterling between official and unofficial may be partly a matter of official policy; but where important changes in private holdings represent policy changes of overseas monetary authorities these can often be explicitly recognized as such. For example, part of the help given to sterling by the European monetary authorities in the spring of 1961 (the so-called Basle arrangements) took the form of increases in *unofficial* holdings of sterling. The amounts involved were given in the official accounts and go below the market-balance line. One may not always be able to make such distinctions explicit; on the other hand it is strongly arguable that the bulk of privately-held sterling balances are very similar to much of what is included under 'miscellaneous short-term capital' in that they are susceptible or not to interest-rate differentials and confidence effects in much the same way.

A different distinction between sterling holdings which might have much to recommend it has now been made possible by the new series of external liabilities and claims in sterling which has been developed by the Bank of England.[10] As well as providing a more useful classification of central monetary institutions, the new series distinguishes between different types of U.K. liability and claim—e.g. current and deposit accounts, Treasury bills, government stock and commercial bills, &c. It may prove possible as we see how the various items move to make a workable division between 'banking' liabilities and

[10] *Bank of England Quarterly Bulletin,* June 1963.

claims (which would go below the line) and 'commercial' liabilities and claims (which would go above it).

'Basic' and 'volatile' changes

Now what is the point of all this? Lumping movements of volatile short-term claims and liabilities in with current receipts and payments and long-term capital movements will simply blur an important distinction, one may urge. Surely an 'overall' deficit of £200 million together with a private monetary inflow of £300 million would represent a greatly inferior position to that of an 'overall' surplus of £100 million and no net private monetary movements? Yet they would both imply a 'market' surplus of £100 million.

This view of the accounts is strikingly illustrated by a comment made in the statistical appendix on the balancing item in the *National Institute Economic Review* for February 1962 which has already been referred to. Pointing out that the balancing item was currently running at over £200 million a year and that the overall deficit in the years 1959–61 averaged at least £300 million, the author of the article concludes: 'Thus the balance of payments can be regarded as anything from indifferent to potentially disastrous according to the view taken of the balancing item' (p. 58). In other words, if the explanation of the discrepancy in the statistics is that the net outflow of long-term capital has been overestimated, the balance of payments is *really* much better than it seems; but if the net outflow of short-term capital has been underestimated, the balance of payments is *really* much worse than it seems.

Obviously there is something in this view. There is a proper sense in which one can say that in 1960 (when the current deficit was £300 million, the 'overall' recorded deficit was £500 million, and the reserves rose by £177 million) some nasty cracks in the situation were being 'papered over'. The paper broke early in 1961 when there was an outflow of short-term funds of almost unprecedented dimensions and a major crisis for sterling. Obviously it would have been misleading here to have looked only at the market balance. But then it is always likely to be misleading to look at only one division of the accounts. Policy-makers must study all the items in the accounts and their interrelationships. However, within the limits of what can be achieved by shifting the emphasis on to a particular way of looking at the balance of payments there are some important advantages which the market balance possesses and the 'overall' balance does not.

First, there is the relatively technical point that one is no longer bothered by the ambiguity of the balancing item. None of the items in the compensatory or official financing account is subject to any significant margin of error. One is still in the dark as to the relative sizes of the components of the market balance, but not as to the size of that balance itself.

Secondly, one no longer has to make an important distinction between long-term and short-term capital. It is widely recognized that any classification distinguishing between these two categories is not merely bound to be arbitrary but is likely not to coincide at all well with how the owners of the assets concerned regard them and behave. As we have already noted, short-term highly marketable assets may be turned over again and again; while equities and long-term debt may be bought and sold for speculative reasons when there is heavy international speculation in favour of or against a particular currency. Long-term is as long-term does.

However, the main argument for a market balance is wider than this. It is not only some forms of so-called long-term capital that are volatile: almost *all* items in the current and long-term capital accounts are potentially volatile: or at least may change substantially fairly quickly. More important, most of them are subject to temporary, cyclical, or otherwise easily reversible changes. They may be influenced in varying degrees and with varying speeds of response by government (not necessarily U.K. government) policies—fiscal, monetary, direct control, &c. The case for emphasizing this similarity of most items in the market balance, at the cost of blurring some obvious and important distinctions, is that too often temporary improvements or deteriorations in the current or long-term capital balances have been regarded as basic changes. Too seldom in discussing or applying balance-of-payments policies has the important distinction been made between policies which do, or may reasonably be hoped to, change the underlying position, and those which merely rephase receipts and payments—which buy or lose time.

This distinction is the subject of the next section.

TABLE I

U.S. Balance of Payments, 1958–61, on two alternative classifications

($ billion)

A. *Official U.S. classification*

	1958–9 Avge.	1960–1 Avge.
Payments	28.6	31.6
Imports of goods & services	22.1	23.1
Remittances & pensions	.8	.9
U.S. govt. grants & credits	3.1	3.7
U.S. private long-term capital	2.5	2.5
U.S. private short-term capital	.2	1.4
Receipts	24.5	29.0
Exports of goods & services	23.3	27.6
Repayments on U.S. govt. loans	.8	1.0
Foreign capital, excl. liquid funds	.4	.4
Errors & omissions	.4	—.6
Balance on above items ['the deficit']	—3.6	—3.2

Items measuring change in 'net international liquidity'	1958–9 Avge.	1960–1 Avge.
Official holdings of gold & convertible currencies	1.5	1.2
Liquid liabilities to foreign & international monetary authorities	1.2	1.2
Liquid liabilities to foreign & commercial banks & other private or international holders	1.0	.8

B. *Suggested 'basic balance' classification*

Payments	28.4	30.2
Imports of goods & services	22.1	23.1
Remittances & pensions	.8	.9
U.S. govt. grants & credits	3.1	3.7
U.S. private long-term capital	2.5	2.5
Receipts	24.5	28.9
Exports of goods & services	23.3	27.6
Repayments on U.S. govt. loans	.8	1.0
Foreign long-term investment in U.S.	.4	.4
'Basic' balance	−3.9	−1.2
Monetary movements :		
Official holdings of gold & convertible currencies	1.5	1.2
Liquid liabilities to foreign & international monetary authorities	1.2	1.2
Liquid liabilities to foreign & commercial banks & other private or international holders	1.0	.8
U.S. private short-term capital net	−.1	−1.4
Errors & omissions	.4	−.6

Source: Lary, Table A-1 (p. 140).

TABLE 2

U.K. Balance of Payments, 1958–62

(£ million)

A. *Official classification*

	1958	1959	1960	1961	1962
Current balance	+342	+140	−272	−34	+74
*Long-term capital**					
Net intergovernmental loans	−44	−118	−92	−16	−91
U.K. subscriptions to IMF, IFC, IDA, & European Fund	—	−236	−10	−9	−9
Other official long-term capital net	−6	−2	—	−20	−5
Private investment:	−133	−131	−185	+91	+15
outward	−298	−307	−313	−326	−259
inward	+165	+176	+228	+417	+274
Total long-term capital	−183	−487	−187	+46	−90
Balance on current & long-term capital account	+159	−347	−459	+12	−16
Balancing item	+43	−58	+269	+8	+115
*Monetary movements**	−202	+405	+190	−20	−99
Miscellaneous capital	+11	+33	+145	−62	+115
Change in overseas sterling holdings	+58	+236	+220	+72	−398
U.K. balance in EPU	−10	+9	—	—	—
Official holdings of non-convertible currencies	+23	+8	+2	+1	+1
Gold & convertible currency reserves	−284	+119	−177	−31	+183

* An increase in assets or a decrease in liabilities is shown as *minus*.
A decrease in assets or an increase in liabilities is shown as *plus*.
Thus in 1958 the reserves *rose* by £284 million.

B. *'Market balance'* classification*

	1958	1959	1960	1961	1962
Private balance					
Current	+566	+373	+15	+302	+441
Long-term capital	−133	−131	−85	+91	+15
Miscellaneous short-term capital	+11	+33	+145	−62	+115
Unofficial sterling balances	+197	+56	+338	−346	+61
Total private balance	+641	+331	+413	−15	+632
Govt. 'non-compensatory' balance†					
Military	−130	−133	−175	−202	−229
Economic aid (current & capital)	−74	−99	−105	−122	−122
Other	−43	−48	−55	−61	−63
Total Govt. 'non-compensatory' balance	−247	−280	−335	−385	−414
Balancing item	+43	−58	+269	+8	+115
'Market balance'	+437	−7	+347	−392	+333
Compensatory finance					
U.K. subscriptions to IMF, IFC, IDA, & European Fund	—	−236	−10	−9	−9
Official long-term capital excl. economic aid†	−27	−73	−44	+13	−49
U.K. balance in EPU	−10	+9	—	—	—
Changes in official sterling holdings	−139	+180	−118	+418	−459
Official holdings of non-convertible currencies	+23	+8	+2	+1	+1
Gold and convertible currency reserves	−284	+119	−177	−31	+183

* Throughout the table, an increase in assets or a decrease in liabilities is shown as *minus*; a decrease in assets or increase in liabilities is shown as *plus*. Thus in 1958 the reserves *rose* by £284 million.

† These items are somewhat crudely distinguished. For 'economic aid' I have simply added to the figures for *current* economic aid (*U.K. Balance of Payments 1963*, Table 8) the net intergovernmental loan position with all areas other than North America and Western Europe. For military expenditure I have added 'other transfers' to the official figures for net military expenditure (see note on 'other transfers' in *U.K. Balance of Payments 1963*). The official statisticians would be able to draw the distinctions I wish to draw much more precisely than I have done.

3

Rephasing and Readjustment

OFFICIAL policies for adjusting the balance of payments
are usually classified in terms of means—monetary, fiscal,
exchange control, &c—or in terms of the particular items
in the balance of payments they are intended to affect. The
suggestion I have been leading up to in the last section is
that these distinctions be downgraded somewhat in favour
of a distinction in terms of the degree of permanence of
their effect. Over-simply, we may distinguish two kinds of
policy: those that buy time (rephasing), and those that
change the situation (readjusting). The second group
might be subdivided into those that change expectations,
including confidence effects, and those that change real
economic magnitudes. The distinctions cannot be un-
ambiguously made: the line between buying a great deal
of time and effecting a change in the situation which is not
absolutely permanent is blurry; and some actions will both
buy time and change the situation. However, the distinction is useful because it concentrates attention on what is
actually being achieved (or can be hoped to be achieved)
by a given policy and what is not.

Buying time

The most obvious way of buying time is by financing a
deficit instead of reducing it. (Indeed, it might be thought
that the distinction between buying time and changing the
situation was simply the more familiar one between

financing and reducing a deficit. But this is not so as we shall see in a minute.) In the simplest case we can tide over accidental or seasonal fluctuations in the market balance by letting the reserves run up or down. That is what they are for. We may also be able to ride out a stock cycle—and perhaps an even more deep-seated business cycle—provided (and they are two big provisos) that the reserves are big enough and that the cycles can be recognized at the time for what they are.

In practice, the U.K. can only buy a very small amount of time with her reserves. Once the rate of fall of the reserves reaches any size this will of itself tend to worsen the market balance, through leads and lags and short-term capital movements, because it will alter expectations for the worse.[1] A rise in liabilities will give considerably more time than a fall in reserves—even if the basic difference between the two situations is the relatively fortuitous one of whether the deficit is with the sterling or the non-sterling area. This is for two reasons. First, there is the statistical accident that figures for sterling holding are published only quarterly, and nearly a quarter in arrears, while the figure for the reserves is published monthly within a day or two of the end of the month, and the exchange rate is published daily. Thus a rapid deterioration which is appearing as an increase of liabilities will not be so immediately or easily seen, and hence may not lead so quickly to cumulative confidence effects.

More important, there is a basic asymmetry between a fall in reserves and a rise in liabilities: the reserves cannot fall below zero while there is no clearly definable upper limit beyond which the liabilities cannot go. This means that a

[1] Of course, the authorities are not entirely passive even in the very short term. They have every day to make tactical decisions as to how far to let strength or weakness show in the exchange rate and how far in the reserves. Within narrow limits, they can, according as their policies are well or ill advised, extend or reduce the time that can be bought by the reserves.

C

fall in reserves is in a real sense more serious than a corresponding rise in liabilities. Suppose the reserves are £1,000 million and short-term liabilities are £4,000 million. Then if a deficit of £600 million is financed out of the reserves, the liquid asset-liability ratio will have deteriorated from 1 : 4 to 1 : 10 and a further similar deficit *could not* be financed from the reserves. On the other hand if the deficit is financed by an increase in liabilities the ratio will deteriorate only from 1 : 4 to 1 : 4.6 and a further similar deficit *could* be financed from the reserves. Thus the way in which the deficit is financed could influence the amount of time bought even if there were no confidence-induced movements at all. Where speculative movements are a major consideration, the way in which the deficit is financed can influence the length of time effectively bought quite substantially. In recent years the Americans have often spoken very feelingly to the Europeans on this asymmetry and its effects in practice on the U.S. payments position.[2]

When the financing is effected through an increase in liabilities, as a result of deliberate 'compensatory' policies by foreign or international authorities—i.e. when we are able to borrow through Basle-type measures (see p. 97) or from the IMF—the time bought may be much longer again. This is partly because there will be some kind of definite undertaking as to how long the finance is provided for (whereas in an increase in liabilities to other countries arising out of normal commercial and monetary transactions there is no such undertaking) and in the case of the IMF this may be several years. There will also be important confidence effects, as this sort of financing will normally be seen as reflecting a decision (which can be implemented) not to devalue—at least for some time.

[2] See, for example, the speech made by Mr Roosa, U.S. Treasury Under-Secretary, to the American Bankers' Association in May 1962.

There will in addition probably be confidence effects stemming from the measures taken as a condition of getting the credit.

Instead of, or as well as, financing a market deficit until by some means or other it is rectified, the authorities may buy the necessary time by taking measures which reduce one or other part of the total deficit for a short time. The improvement as a result of such measures will not be lasting, but if they are successful it will not be reversed until a more fundamental improvement has taken place. The most obvious way of doing this is to induce an inflow of short-term capital by higher interest rates, with the idea that by the time this inflow has died down or begun to reverse itself, other elements in the market will have improved.

So far, so familiar. It is self-evident that running down the reserves or borrowing from the IMF simply buys time; and it is pretty obvious that attracting money with high interest rates will usually do the same. But it is sometimes forgotten how much of the effect of what appear to be more 'fundamental' balance-of-payments measures is simply to buy time. Take, for example, the policy of cutting back home demand which has been followed in the U.K. in one form or another in all the balance-of-payments crises since the war. This has usually had a significant effect on the current balance fairly quickly, but most of such effects have been through reducing imports; and much of the import reductions has in fact derived from reduced investment in imported stocks. Then when demand rose again there was a more than proportional increase in investment in stocks. Instead of the traditional approach of using the reserves as a cushion for a stock cycle, the authorities have engendered stock cycles as a cushion for the reserves. Even where the effect of cutting back demand means that certain imports are never taken (as opposed to being simply postponed), this may not imply any genuine correction of the underlying position. If when demand expands once more the propensity to import continues unchanged—so that imports are merely taken (say) one year later than they otherwise would have been—we cannot say that the market balance has been in any way improved. We have simply sacrificed a year's growth (say) for a once-for-all improvement in our reserves, or asset-liability position. This may be worth doing, but it is *not* in itself putting our balance of payments right. Only if demand (in relation to supplies) is henceforth permanently to be lower than its crisis level; or, alternatively, if lasting changes are produced in our relative costs and prices or in our propensities to import or export out of income can we say that demand reduction has been a corrective rather than a time-buying measure (see section 4).

Similarly with import or exchange controls. Only if the imposition or tightening of these is meant to be semi-permanent; or if new and better patterns of production and trade are set up as a result of the temporary control, can it be claimed that they are more than time-buying. The experience of Australia and New Zealand in the 1950s show how far repeated imposition and relaxation of import controls can result simply in rephasing imports. Importers come increasingly to buy in excess of current need when restrictions are relaxed, (*a*) to make good stocks run down during the period of restriction; (*b*) to build up stocks against the possibility of future restrictions; and (*c*) if quotas tend to be based on imports in the previous period, to make sure of as big a quota as possible when restrictions are next imposed. This is not necessarily a criticism of import restrictions; when a country is confronted with very large fluctuations in her export receipts which are beyond her control—as Australia and New

Zealand have been[3]—it may be the most sensible way of coping with the balance of payments; any inefficiencies, inequities, and long-run deleterious effects of the restrictions being regarded as the price to be paid for the smoothing-out effects.

Finally, even the most drastic, most 'fundamental' of all balance-of-payments policies—altering the exchange rate—can be thought of as a time-buying measure. One might, in certain circumstances, believe that the cost-inflationary consequences of devaluing would mean that its beneficial effects on the balance of payments would be more or less wiped out in say four or five years, and yet recommend a devaluation, on the ground that it would give you more time, freer of strings, in which to take fundamental corrective action than any other kind of action. A view something like this appears to have been held (though not quite in the crude form given here) by the National Institute of Economic Research over the past few years. This is obviously a tenable position in principle, but one would have to bear in mind that the inflationary pressures generated in the years that had been bought might make some fundamental corrective actions (e.g. an incomes policy) harder to take.

'Fundamental' changes

If so many measures can be said to be wholly or partly time-buying in effect, what measures are there to make lasting adjustments to the balance of payments? What are the things one can do with the time that one cay buy in so many ways?

We can say that anything that changes prices, costs, techniques, inventiveness, tastes, attitudes, and the long-run average relationship between home capacity and

[3] And if she can rely on your trading partners not to retaliate.

home demand may influence the market balance in a lasting way: although of course there may be several conflicting effects of a given measure, and any improvement secured in the long-run market balance may be very costly in terms of unemployment and/or slow growth.

Carried out with appropriate supporting policies, a devaluation can certainly effect a long-lasting change in costs and prices relative to those of other countries: this is discussed in some detail in Section 5. Although, as we have seen, in some circumstances a policy of deflation may simply buy time, there is no doubt that in others it can effect a fundamental change. There have been so many arguments about the effects of deflationary policies—and so many people have talked at cross purposes—that the subject demands to be considered at some length. It is accordingly also taken up again in Section 4.

Exchange control—whether over imports or capital movements—may provide a readjustment instead of the replacement that we have already seen is quite common. This subject links naturally with wider questions about capital flows and is dealt with briefly, together with tariffs, in Section 6.

There are a host of other readjusting policies whose merits have been greatly discussed and we shall not spend much time on them.[4] They fall roughly into two categories: those aimed at improving the economy generally and those aimed directly at the receipts and payments that make up the balance of payments.

Tuning up the Economy

Among the overall improving policies are the following. *Incomes policy.* I do not intend to add to the mountains of

[4] Many of them are well dealt with in the two NEDC reports, *Conditions favourable to faster growth* (1963) and *Export Trends* (1963).

material already written on the possibilities and difficulties of an incomes policy. The difficulties are enormous,
but there is no doubt in my mind that this is the only way
properly to tackle cost inflation; and that for the U.K. it
offers the best chance of radically improving the relative
competitiveness and hence her balance of payments. This
is largely because I think it should prove possible to
introduce an incomes policy in this country well before
any of our main competitors get round to adopting one.

However, an incomes policy, even when it has been
adopted, will take time to produce an improvement in the
external balance. It would be optimistic to hope that it
would make possible any substantial or widespread *reduction* in prices. Thus if our costs and prices are out of line
with those of other countries the direct effect of the policy
will depend on other countries' continuing to inflate: our
prices, it is hoped, will rise more slowly than those elsewhere. There will be secondary effects: the reduction or
cessation of inflation may significantly improve the market
balance by improving confidence in the economy and the
currency; and it may be possible to pursue more vigorous
and sustained growth policies, which will themselves
improve the balance of payments through their stimulus
to investment and technological advance. All these things
will take time.

Increasing competition. Intensified anti-monopoly or anti-
restrictive practices policies must run the gauntlet of a
double scepticism: first that competition can be legisla-
tively enforced; and secondly that there will be a net benefit from any extra competition that *is* enforced. Tariff
reduction could certainly provide extra competition and,
provided it were not too sudden, might give great stimulus
to the economy; but any improvement to the balance of
payments would probably be some time in coming, even
if the tariff reductions were multilateral. If our industries

need the stimulus of foreign competition then presumably a reduction in tariffs both here and abroad will mean that imports will rise faster than exports to begin with. Thus the balance of payments may get worse before it gets better.

Increasing research, investment, &c. There are a number of ways in which the government can help increase research, investment, and the pace of technological change: fiscal incentives such as investment allowances, free depreciation, and (possibly) a pay-roll tax; more governmentally supported research; facilitating the transmission of knowledge of best practices through industry; setting up fighting firms in particular industries, &c.

Improving labour and labour mobility. The government can help here by fostering and working for improved redundancy schemes, transfer grants for workers, higher unemployment benefits, developing new growth points for the economy by appropriate public investment policies, and in many other ways. This is a very important field where much good can be done—but once again it will take time.

Indicative planning. The whole range of activities covered by the phrase 'indicative planning'—the development of industrial commissions on the French model, the working out of interlocking targets and the rationalizing of investment decisions—should make a substantially faster rate of growth compatible with a reasonably satisfactory average balance of payments, over a period of years.

Tackling the balance of payments itself

As well as, or instead of, policies to tune up the whole economy, the government may direct its attention to the balance-of-payments sector itself. Many of the policies already mentioned, for example, may be carried out in specific relation to the balance of payments. Thus fiscal incentives to investment may discriminate between exporting and non-exporting industries; semi-concealed subsidies may be given to exports, such as a value-added tax which is rebated for exporters; measures to improve the quality or mobility of labour or to increase research may all operate discriminatorily between sectors which contribute directly to improving the balance of payments and those that do not.

This approach may often be valid and useful, but it carries great dangers. There has been a marked tendency in the U.K., for example, for successive governments to favour more exports, *tout court*.[5] Such policies, even if successful, can in principle worsen the balance of payments. An increase of £10 million in the exports of one commodity may cost £4 million in imports and an increase of £9 million in the exports of another commodity may only cost £2 million in imports. Or the exports achieved may be at the expense of investment which would soon have produced a much greater stream of exports. Import-saving measures have not had the sex-appeal of export-increasing ones though they might in some cases have been more beneficial. Incentives—such as subsidies for investment &c.—for 'exporters' may discriminate in a pointless and distorting way between the last and the second-last stages of the production process: subsidies for exports may lead to supply difficulties for the exporters of motor-cars as the manufacturers of motor-car components switch to exporting a greater proportion of their output.

The marginal contribution to the balance of payments of any particular increase in exports will never be known with any certainty or accuracy— or not at least until the statistics are a good deal better than they are at present.

---

[5] A good example of this very naïve economics is the exports 'gateway' in the Restrictive Practices Act.

There is a *prima facie* case, therefore, for aiming policies more at improving the general competitive position of the economy—in terms of costs and prices, product quality, inventiveness, flexibility—rather than concentrating on particular gimmicks to encourage business to export.

There is likely to be no harm, however, and there may be some good, in working to remove or lessen individual supply limitations on exports by providing export-credit guarantees; easier finance for exporters; fostering exporting organizations which can take care of the advertising, handling of importing agencies, freight, insurance, paperwork, &c., involved in exporting for a large number of small firms. This last may be a promising line of approach though the high proportion of U.K. exports which comes from a relatively small number of large firms may suggest that there is more to be gained more easily by increasing the proportion of the output of these identifiable (and therefore individually approachable) firms which is exported, than by sweating to get a little more out of each of an enormous number of small concerns.

Two further ways of acting on individual elements in the balance of payments may be mentioned.

Reduction of government overseas payments

Suggestions to act directly on the balance of payments by restricting private imports or capital flows are discussed in Section 6. What about reducing government payments abroad—grants, loans, or expenditure on goods and services?

The first point to be remembered applies to cutting any government expenditure and is, when stated baldly, trite: care should be taken to see that the gains from the cut outweigh the losses. Many people believe that you can cut any government programme by 5 or 10 per cent without any loss—indeed that you will get a *better* programme as well as saving some money for other things. You will, as the phrase is, be 'cutting out the fat'. This view rests on two assumptions of which certainly one and probably both are unwarranted. First, that there is always 5 or 10 per cent of inefficiency or 'fat' in any programme. This may be true, but I doubt it. There are many government programmes which are ill-conceived, wrongly devised, wholly mistaken; there is much government expenditure which should be reduced, just as there is much which should be expanded. Inefficiency on a major scale there undoubtedly is; but the normal action of Treasury control makes inefficiency on a minor scale much less likely. Most private businesses would have more of this 5 or 10 per cent fat than the average government department.

The second assumption is that if the fat exists, then cutting the programme by 5 or 10 per cent means that what you cut is the fat. This is certainly false. What in fact you cut, nine times out of ten, is morale, efficiency, and part of the programme. If any general principle can be laid down on these matters it should be that no government programme should ever be cut by *less* than 30 per cent. In this way one might hope to avoid some of the ambiguity and hypocrisy involved in cuts like the 10 per cent reduction in expenditure on the foreign service in 1961. To cut anything by 30 per cent or more a government must know itself to be making, and be seen to be making, a policy decision. However, all this, though it has some relevance to the balance of payments, is really a step into a quite different subject, the control of public expenditure. It is a digression, prompted by spleen.

To return to the balance of payments, we have already noted that cutting any juicy-looking payment somewhere in the accounts is bound to involve some reduction in an apparently unconnected receipt somewhere else. The net

saving is always less than the gross saving, and it is the net
saving which counts. The two main government items are
defence and aid—currently running at about £250 million
and £150 million respectively. Estimating the true saving
to the balance of payments of cutting either of these can be
a very complicated exercise in hunting down opportunity
cost. Out of a grant of £x million to a particular country,
how much is spent on British exports? How much would
total expenditure by that country be reduced if the grant
was not made? Is there an unsatisfied demand from other
countries for these exports which could become effective
if they were not sent to the grant-receiving country? What
is the import content of the aid-stimulated exports? Is
there excess capacity in the economy? Could the resources
engaged in producing the aid-stimulated exports be
switched to output, making a larger net contribution to
the balance of payments? And so on. Some calculations
along these lines are almost certainly attempted in Whitehall with respect to aid, where in so far as there is an outside lobby at all it is pressing for an *increase* in U.K. aid;
it is the Treasury who set an upper limit to aid programmes, primarily in terms of balance-of-payments cost.
But there is no indication whether such calculations are
made about the defence programme. If they are not they
certainly should be.

Once we can assess the true balance-of-payments cost of
defence or aid expenditure we must set this against the
social gain of the programme. Too often one hears a false
separation made between cost and benefit: 'We must
frame our defence policies in the light of our overall
defence needs and international commitments: we cannot
prejudice national security for the sake of a few million
pounds on the balance of payments.'

But we don't spend the entire national income on
defence. There is no such thing as an absolute need for a

certain sum: there are simply at every level of expenditure gains and losses from spending more. Ideally a programme should be at that level where the gains from spending any more on it would be just offset by the losses. A defence programme allegedly geared to our overall defence needs will in practice simply be geared to last year's programme, to the balance of power within the Defence Department, and to various relatively arbitrary criteria and conventions. Introducing and giving full weight to the balance-of-payments cost could only improve the decisions taken. Of course it may be that this is already done; that if it had not been for very strong emphasis placed on the balance-of-payments cost of our overseas defence, expenditure would be even higher than it already is. We cannot tell, but it is hard not to be suspicious.

Thirdly, it is sometimes argued[6] that it is not worth trying to reduce overseas defence expenditure because the gain, if any, will be once-for-all, not continuing. This seems to me a misapprehension. Certainly, if we effect a £50 million net saving on defence expenditure, payments will only once be reduced by £50 million, thereafter staying constant, but this is not the point. If we are currently running an overall or market surplus of £100 million a year, with defence expenditure (net) averaging £200 million, and we reduce defence expenditure by £50 million net, then *ceteris paribus* the surplus from now on (not just in the first year) will average £150 million.

Attracting short-term funds

Private monetary movements are usually thought of as the temporary, volatile element in the balance of payments *par excellence*. Is there anything to be said about them in the context of 'fundamental' or semi-permanent changes?

[6] See a letter to *The Times* of 1 April. 1963 by Professor Thomas Wilson.

For what it is worth, private monetary movements have shown a distinctly improving trend. Reported movements of 'unofficial sterling balances' and 'miscellaneous capital' taken together show an average annual *outflow* of £8 million in the period 1955–8 followed by an average annual *inflow* of £85 million in 1959–62. Moreover, the reported figures undoubtedly understate the net monetary inflow, as the balancing item has averaged about £80 million a year over the past eight years and much of this figure is likely to represent unreported short-term capital inflows (see p. 16). Even if we assume that only half the balancing item represents unreported short-term capital inflows, we see that over the eight-year period 1955–62 there was an average annual monetary inflow of nearly £80 million: £30 million a year in 1955–8 and £125 million a year in 1959–62. Obviously this may not last. Obviously the second period has been dominated by the weakness of the dollar. But the pound itself was weak for part of the period. It is neither in principle, nor historically, out of the question to have a constant net inflow of short-term capital. The main prerequisites of such a situation would presumably be that (*a*) some interest-rate differential was on average maintained compared with other financial centres; (*b*) the market for funds was better diversified, better organized, and provided more opportunities than markets elsewhere; and (*c*) that confidence in the currency was maintained.

The first two prerequisites might very easily apply to sterling and the City of London for some time to come. Of course, if a given market balance is being maintained in this way, it will be reduced not merely if the funds start going out again, but if the rate at which they are coming in begins to drop. With an item as volatile as this it might therefore be thought inappropriate to speak of effecting any sort of basic change simply by maintaining a differential of returns and opportunities for lenders. However, if improved arrangements are made for maintaining confidence in the currency—or quickly allaying weakness in confidence should it occur—as I believe to be both practicable and likely, perhaps one may be able to regard the short-term capital account as a possible source of basic improvement in the market balance. The real lesson of the last few years may not be how quickly short-term funds can first come in and then go out, but how quickly, once appropriate steps are taken, they can be induced to come back once again: how large the net inflow over this period of violent movements actually was.

I don't want to overstate the case. I am not concerned to argue that monetary movements are not, at least potentially, volatile. Only that they are not so much more volatile than other elements in the account.

4

Deflation

DEMAND reduction is claimed to help the balance of payments fundamentally by affecting either or both prices or incomes. More unemployment and excess capacity are claimed to mean (a) lower costs and prices relative to the rest of the world; (b) reduced home demand for imports; (c) reduced home demand for exportable goods and hence greater ability or inducement for producers to meet (or find) foreign orders. Against this view it has been argued (a) that unit costs may rise rather than fall when demand is reduced because unchanged overhead costs must be borne by a smaller output; and (b) that it ignores crucially important dynamic effects, militating against long-run growth of supply, technical change, cost reduction, and general competitive advantage. The arguments on both sides are very familiar to anyone who has glanced in even the most casual way at the economic journalism of the past six or seven years. But despite the frequency with which the arguments have been bandied about, there is frequent confusion in the way they are expressed or opposed to each other; and very little evidence has been adduced on either side.

A narrow range

The first thing to get clear is that it is only the variation of the level of demand within a quite small range that is at issue. If we could devise a genuinely unambiguous and acceptable indication of the level of aggregate demand relative to aggregate supply in the economy, there would be some level beyond which nobody thought demand ought to go; or, to put it another way, down to at least which *everybody* would agree that demand would have to be brought if it had by accident risen higher. However much we wish to emphasize the interdependence of aggregate demand and supply, however strongly we wish to argue that the way to get growth is to keep demand at any one time high in relation to potential output at that time, there will be a limit beyond which this argument will cease to have any further force and where inefficiencies, frustrations, distortions, and balance-of-payments considerations (however masked by devalutations, import controls, &c.) will become pre-eminent. On the other hand there will also be an agreed lower limit below which no one will want demand to fall in relation to potential supply—however much we emphasize the desirability of more labour mobility, lower pressure for wage increases, and the cold winds of competition.

The range between these two levels is quite narrow. For example, if we take as a measure of the relation between supply and demand the unemployment percentage, probably few people would seriously urge that this figure should consistently be much below 1 per cent, and equally few that it should be consistently much above 3 per cent. Of course the unemployment percentage is a very crude indicator of the state of demand. For any given percentage for the country as a whole there is plenty of scope for argument about the effects and significance of variations between regions or industries, between seasonal and structural unemployment, between the relative proportions of skilled and unskilled, old and young, short-term and long-term unemployment. More fundamentally, one can argue about whether the employment figures move with the degree of utilization of physical capacity in the

D

economy—and if they do not, which is the more appropriate measure of the pressure of demand.

Arguments over the adequacy of particular indicators of the pressure of demand are conceptually separable from disputes over the pressure that is appropriate, though in practice they are hopelessly entangled with them. Moreover there are other issues to be sorted out.

Changes versus levels

Most of those who discuss the issue are guilty at one time or another of confusing the effects of a given pressure of demand with the effects of a *change* in that pressure. Thus it is often pointed out that British exports have done relatively poorly when home demand was falling and relatively well when it was rising (e.g. compare 1958 with 1959); and it is sometimes believed that this disposes of the case for a relatively low level of demand in the interests of exports. Nothing could be farther from the case.

Changes in costs, prices, incomes, and import propensities are always taking place in other countries and the effects of these on British exports may dwarf and outweigh those of changes in the pressure of demand at home. However, this kind of difficulty in establishing *any* hypothesis is ubiquitous in economics: it is what makes the subject so fascinating to economists and so infuriating to laymen.

More important to the present argument, the history of the British economy since the war consists rather of successive attempts to change the pressure of demand than of a succession of periods of different, persisting pressures. Up to a point this is inevitable and right. It is a basic aim and responsibility of a modern government to try to keep the economy on a steady path; but in the present state of knowledge it is impossible to keep a large and complex economy from wandering off the path from time to time; and perhaps it always will be. We must expect and require that for most of the time the government will have its foot on either the accelerator or the brake. Thus much of the criticism of 'Stop-Go' is misguided. What is at issue (or should be) is not whether the government should at different times be trying to increase or reduce demand, but the speed and force with which it should react in either direction; and the level of demand *around which* any unavoidable fluctuations should take place.

The government can be criticized (and often has been)[1] for the *magnitude* of its zigzags in the past decade. Demand should never have been allowed (let alone encouraged) to reach the level it did by mid-1955. Once it had reached that level some deflation was necessary; but the prolonged ham-handed deflation that in fact took place in the following three years could only have been justified by an intention to work at a lower average level of demand. It was made nonsense of by the Budget of 1959 which very quickly restored demand to a high level. This pleased those who believed that demand should always be relatively high—but then they would not have carried the previous deflation so far. Those who believed that demand should always be relatively low were deprived of any opportunity of demonstrating that they were right or of being shown to be wrong.

As far as the balance of payments is concerned all the government's operations on demand in recent years can characterized as rephasing rather than readjusting. But over the past year or so it looks as if policy may have been at least more consistent. The unemployment level reached during the winter and spring of 1962-3 was clearly greater than the government desired: forecasts proved to

[1] See *inter multa alia* I. M. D. Little, 'Fiscal Policy', in G. D. N. Worswick and P. H. Ady, eds., *The British Economy in the 1950s*, (London, 1963).

be in error and the winter was very severe. If these factors are allowed for, however, it looks as if the government was aiming for a somewhat lower pressure of demand than had previously prevailed. It may be that the expansion which is now under way will take place without restoring demand fully to its previous levels. Then we shall perhaps get some inkling as to the implications of a genuine re-adjustment of the balance of payments by means of the average pressure of demand.

Conflicting views

In so far as the protagonists on either side do distinguish the effects of different average pressures of demand from the effects of changing pressures, there are two main general arguments between them.

First, will a lower level of demand maintained over time permanently improve the balance of payments? Those, like Professor Paish, arguing for a lower level of demand say that it will, (*a*) because prices will rise less or not at all; (*b*) because there will be pressure on businesses to find export markets, since it will be harder for them to sell at home; (*c*) because there will be more 'flexibility' in the economy—more labour mobility, fewer bottlenecks, &c. Some of the opponents of this view challenge at least the first two of these points. They urge that over the relevant variation in pressure of demand, the rate at which prices rise is indeterminate; i.e. that demand-inflation only becomes important at levels of demand higher than they would recommend, while cost-inflation is relatively insen-sitive to the level of demand between say 1 and 3 per cent unemployment. Indeed, they may go farther: since cost-inflation must be dealt with by an incomes policy and since it will be difficult to get an incomes policy accepted if there is significant unemployment, there may turn out to be a slight *inverse* relationship between the level of employment and cost-inflation.

A different, less convincing argument is that a lower pressure of demand actually raises costs and prices since fixed overhead costs have to be spread over a smaller output. This can only have validity over the short run and when demand is being reduced (and even here it is very doubtful whether businessmen do raise their prices in response to an increase in costs of this kind). Over the longer run, if a lower pressure of demand is maintained capacity will be at least partially adjusted to this demand; and even if capacity is from now on significantly less utilized than before, this could only produce a once-for-all increase in costs.

Similarly one may argue that the view that businessmen will be forced to export because the home market has become more difficult also applies primarily to the once-for-all changes while demand is being reduced. Once full adaptation to the lower level of demand has taken place it is not clear that there will continue to be a stimulus to export. On the other hand the opposing argument, that it is only on the basis of a flourishing home market that manufacturers can afford to develop the essentially marginal business of exporting, appears in the same way to depend on a change in climate rather than a persistent climate of a particular kind.

Once one distinguishes carefully between a given pressure of demand and a change in it, most of the argument in fact centres on a dispute whether a high or a low pressure of demand is better for growth. The Paish view is that it is possible to grow faster in the long run at a lower level of demand because the economy will not be held back from time to time by balance-of-payments crises and will be more flexible. One opposing view is that if enough stimulus is given to the economy to make it grow the

pressure of demand will automatically rise to a relatively
high level: or to put it the other way round, that only in
the climate of high demand will growth-producing decisions—to expand, to modernize, to do research, &c.—be
taken. Hence, also, this argument runs, only if demand is
high will the balance of payments ultimately improve.

This last view too—that the deflationists have a static
view of the economy and neglect dynamic factors—has
obviously much force in the context of a demand *reduction*;
but perhaps less force in the context of a persistently maintained lower level of demand—provided that the economy
as a whole is expanding. It might well be possible in a
context of increasing public investment programmes and
co-ordinated private investment plans under the aegis of
NEDC to secure the expectation of sustained growth that
is necessary to induce growth-producing decisions, at a
number of different pressures of demand.

Conflict of ends

A final argument between the expansionists and the
deflationists is on a different level. It concerns a difference
in the importance attached to maintaining a very high
level of employment for its own sake. This is sometimes
expressed as a conflict between employment and the
balance of payments. It would certainly be indefensible to
prefer a sound balance of payments for its own sake to a
higher level of employment: the balance of payments is a
means, not an end, as we have pointed out before. The
only rational conflict can be between faster growth (which
the deflationists see as *depending* on a sounder balance of
payments) and high employment. Here the dispute can be
about the facts: which way do you get faster growth? But
it can also be about value-judgements: do you prefer
slightly higher growth and slightly lower employment or

vice versa? It may be that many people would be prepared
to sacrifice a little growth to maintain higher employment
if the alternatives were squarely presented. If so, this may
be a dispute which cannot be settled by the evidence.

Some reconciliation might be brought about, however, by
higher unemployment benefits, by more training schemes,
and more inducements to labour mobility. If unemployment involved less hardship and were less futile one might
be prepared to see slightly more of it in the immediate
interest of the balance of payments and the longer-run
interest of growth.

5

Devaluation

THE subtle and inflammatory subject of the exchange rate can no longer be postponed. We have already noted that a devaluation of the currency can sometimes be regarded as a way of buying a good deal of time to do other things. For such a purpose it has the advantage that the time bought is on one's own terms: when one borrows funds, the lender—be he private or official—is apt to have something to say about what one does with them. On the other hand, as we have already seen, devaluation is likely to produce effects which may conflict with the corrective policies one wishes to pursue. If the cost-inflationary consequences of higher priced imports are substantial the post-devaluation climate might be a poor one for establishing an incomes policy.

In any case devaluation must normally be thought of not as a way of buying time, but as itself a device of adjustment—the correction of last resort to a fundamental deficit in the market balance. It is worth discussing the possibility and consequences of devaluation for the U.K. in some detail. This is partly because the subject needs more thorough airing than it customarily gets; and partly because views taken on this subject are crucially important both tactically and conceptually for the part that sterling can play as a key currency.

The devaluation of sterling is a genuinely explosive subject. No one with any claims to authority or influence can ever admit that the possibility exists. Sir Stafford Cripps, a model of probity, was forced in the summer of 1949 into lying in a more bare-faced way than many a truly devious politician has had to do in his entire career. But the operative word here is 'forced'. It is inherent in the subject that people concerned with it cannot truly discuss it. This may be a pity, but it is part of the logic of the situation and must be accepted.

Unfortunately, however, this fact tends to foster a quite separate attitude to the question. Undiscussibility can be confused with unthinkability. From the correct position that it would be irresponsible for someone in authority to talk publicly of the possible need for the U.K. to devalue it is a short (but illicit) step to the view that it is irresponsible for *anyone* to talk in this way. Hence, for example, the stir over the letters to *The Times* early in 1963 from Mr Nicholas Kaldor and others recommending devaluation, or even, in Mr Kaldor's case, a floating rate. Here, perhaps, the matter was complicated by the fear that it might be thought that Mr Kaldor's views on this subject carried weight with the leaders of the Labour Party. As a result we were treated to the edifying and enjoyable spectacle of Dr Thomas Balogh assuming the statesman's mantle and reproving the irresponsibility of his more volatile colleague.[1]

A second difficulty in discussing devaluation as a real possibility for an actual currency (as opposed to an exercise in one of those mental gymnasiums of theory equipped with lots of elasticities and very few countries) is that there is so much emotional capital invested in the exchange rate.

Irrationality in economics

There is a good book waiting to be written on irrationality in economics.[2] A couple of pages back we spoke of

[1] See his letter to *The Times* of 19 Mar. 1963.

[2] Anyone intending to write it should start by reading Norman O. Brown's brilliant book, *Life against Death* (London, 1959), especially the chapter entitled 'Filthy Lucre'.

the indefensibility of preferring a sound balance of payments for its own sake to high employment for its own sake, though we pointed out that it was quite tenable to prefer it as a means to the eminently rational aim of growth. This is, I think, acceptable within the context in which we usually discuss economics and economic matters; but if we ask ourselves how we really feel about Britain's slow growth rate and why we want it to be faster, we are likely to find, if we are honest, that we *feel* very much on this matter as we do about winning or losing test-matches (though of course we *know* that one subject is trivial and the other important). This is an obvious and superficial example of a deeper phenomenon. All economic behaviour, if one can stand back a pace and rid oneself of the presumption that it is rational, is apt to seem obsessive, arbitrary, and ritualistic. Economists are concerned not to find reasons for this behaviour but to provide rationalizations of it; and the extremes to which we will go are quite extraordinary. Take our necessary invention 'economic man' and the curious way we say that we know he doesn't exist, and that people are really irrational in much of their behaviour. Irrational! If we were ever to meet an economic man it would immediately be apparent to everyone that he was in the grip of a neurosis of quite extraordinary severity.

Prices have particularly strong symbolic value for us all: as witness the strength of the hostility to inflation of so many people who stand to gain economically from it. (We wheel on a stage-army of pensioners for this performance; but we keep it in the wings at all other times: we don't vote to transfer any real resources to the pensioners.) Think how frequently the decline in the value of the pound is brought up *in vacuo* and without reference to incomes; and how wry, sad, nostalgic, frustrated or angry it can make us feel. Our feelings about price changes

it is somehow especially disruptive and unfair to other countries. But in a static context *any* improvement we make in our current balance must adversely affect the balance of our trading partners: the means by which the improvement is made is immaterial. In reality other countries' positions may be improved if we regain equilibrium while expanding incomes and demand provided we do so without too much inflation, while they will be worse off if we do so by deflation and stagnation. It is true that a devaluation has an immediate and obvious effect on the trading community in other countries while deflation has not. Moreover, there will be windfall losses and gains for home and foreign traders using short-term credit; and this could certainly be unsettling and disruptive for a time. But in the longer run, for a given improvement in the balance there could certainly be circumstances in which the effects of devaluation were more beneficial than other measures such as deflation, to the rest of the world.

Wealth effects

So much for the 'trading effects' of devaluation. But the fact that sterling is a reserve currency means that there will be important 'wealth effects' too; and these greatly complicate the picture. First, the liquid asset-liability ratio of the U.K. will be improved. Another way of putting this is, of course, that countries who hold their reserves in sterling will have their liquid wealth—or at least the purchasing power of their liquid wealth outside the sterling area—reduced. Governments and individuals alike might become disenchanted with sterling as a store of value and decide to hold something else—gold or dollars—instead. It is true that this would be shutting the door after the horse had bolted: but then, it might be argued, there might still be another horse inside. Indeed there might. The size of the currency movements that could occur could easily render the position of sterling more dicky than before. Moreover, every conversion into gold would represent a destruction of international liquidity; and a very severe strain might be placed on the dollar. The fact that suspicion of one reserve currency had proved justified would be likely to intensify suspicion of the other. In short, the world's payments system would be very seriously dislocated; a devaluation of the dollar might even be forced on the U.S. authorities. In this case, most other countries would probably follow suit and the original trading benefits be wiped out. Even if massive rescue operations by the IMF and the Europeans, and firmness by the Americans, stabilized the position without devaluation of the dollar, the U.K. might well be worse off than before with much lower reserves, more volatile liabilities and large obligations towards the IMF and the Europeans.

Some of these effects might be mitigated if the value of the sterling balances were 'written up' as the U.K. devalued and simultaneously given a gold guarantee for the future. This avoids some of the difficulties involved in giving a gold guarantee out of the blue (see p. 93). But which sterling balances? If only the official balances there would still be enormous conversion of sterling: privately-held sterling balances amount to about £1,000 million—the same size as the reserves. If these were written up too there would still remain all the other kinds of short-term debt to foreigners not officially counted as sterling balances.[5] More important, if you guarantee the gold value of liabilities to the tune of three times as much gold as you possess, people may doubt whether you will keep your word. Moreover, to the extent that such devices did

---

[5] For example, short-term borrowing overseas by local authorities and hire-purchase companies, borrowing to finance purchases of certain imports, advance payments made against British exports.

help the pound it might be very much at the expense of the dollar—again possibly leading to its devaluation.

Thus, though it seems to me obvious that in an international system of fully independent sovereign states with 'fixed' exchange rates, the possibility should exist for every country to change its own rate—it would be nonsense to expect all rates to remain 'right' for ever, even if one were sure that they were right to start with (which one never is) —nevertheless I believe that as things are the U.K. probably should never devalue. She might of course be driven to it by an overwhelming crisis: but it would be an act of desperation carrying no assurance that it would improve her situation. As a genuine, even if unlikely, alternative to other policies I do not think it has existed for the U.K. since about the middle of the 1950s. (The situation in 1949 was radically different, with extremely tight exchange controls operating in most countries and the European post-war recovery yet to begin.)

This view is based, of course, on a belief as to where the U.K.'s self-interest lies. I do not put it forward because I believe that the U.K. has a moral responsibility towards the holders of sterling or to uphold the world's payments system. That is simply speech-maker's cant. The obligations are in sterling not gold. Moreover, morality is more complicated. Every policy will hurt someone; and in any case if we *could* devalue without greatly disturbing the international-payments mechanism we might be able to expand faster and more than compensate underdeveloped overseas sterling-area countries in increased aid and demand for their products, for the reduction of their liquid assets.

A flexible rate

Everything that has been said so far about exchange alterations has been concerned with changes from one

E

'fixed' rate to another. There is, of course, an alternative policy: letting the rate float. There is certainly much to be said for this policy in principle: treating the exchange rate like any other price, and refusing to administer it, is an appealing idea. However, the crux of the matter lies with the speculators. If a flexible rate did in fact vary at all sharply and at all often, it would be a serious handicap to trade. Those who advocate a flexible rate admit this, but believe that currency speculation will act to stabilize the market. I am more timid. Clearly it might be possible to develop a wide and active enough market to ensure reasonable stability. But then again it might not; or not for some time after the initial decision to float was taken, and in these circumstances a lot of damage could be done, even in the case of a country not operating a reserve currency.

In the U.K.'s case the dangers would be magnified because if the swings were at all large there might be wholesale liquidation of the sterling balances as monetary authorities decided they preferred gold or a more stable currency. It really does seem to be nonsense to have a reserve currency floating—at any rate in a world where other exchange rates are fixed.

Finally, to float would be to act in defiance of all that has been developed in the way of international monetary co-operation since the war. This argument would have no force if we were at the end of our tether—if we were finding that we were getting no help from the IMF or from other monetary authorities. But until we have exhausted the possibilities of the existing framework it would seem to me more constructive and likely to be fruitful to work within it rather than set out on our own.

6

Exchange Control and Capital Movements

'STERLING strong and free'. This anthropomorphic slogan from the fifties (faintly echoing the ill-fated wish to 'look the dollar in the face' of thirty years earlier) raises a number of questions. How free is sterling now? How much freer should it become? How in fact are freedom and strength related?

It seems worth-while to spend a little time setting out a few turgid details of exchange control, contrasting the situation in the U.K. with that in the U.S. on the one hand and the Continental countries on the other. There is to my knowledge no simple account of this; and the general reader, uninterested in such technicalities can easily skip them and rejoin us on p. 74.

In what follows I have leaned heavily on the IMF *Fourteenth Annual Report on Exchange Restrictions* (May 1963) and Claudio Segré, 'Capital Movements in the European Economic Community', *Banca Nazionale de Lavoro Quarterly Review*, March 1962. I hope that the picture given is substantially accurate, but several warnings are appropriate. First, the position is changing all the time; I have tried to include all significant changes which have occurred since the two sources quoted above went to press, but I may not have been successful; and further developments may occur after this has gone to press. Secondly, for movements of funds requiring individual authorization which is not automatically granted, no written description can convey the effective tightness or ease of the control: there is really no substitute for asking the authorities' permission in a number of individual cases and seeing what happens. Thirdly, I have aimed at giving as good a general idea of the overall relative tightness of control in the various countries as I can, and have therefore deliberately ignored many points of technical detail where these seemed to me of only minor significance, obscuring important similarities and differences between countries. Thus those who wish or need to know the precise situation for any particular transaction are referred to the sources already quoted and (especially of course if their own money is likely to be involved) to the exchange-control authorities in the countries concerned.

Current account

This need not delay us long. Imports and exports of goods and services are now practically fully liberalized in the U.K. and the countries of the EEC as well as in the U.S. For *merchandise imports*, foreign exchange is freely available in all eight countries: any restrictions come in with the necessity in various cases to obtain licences to import goods. The main reasons for such restrictions as do exist are political and military: thus the U.K. and the EEC countries all impose restrictions on what might loosely be described as the Sino-Soviet bloc, though the countries included in the bloc vary slightly and the degree of restriction on purchases from it vary considerably. In the U.S. all goods from China, North Korea, and Cuba are subject to licence.

There are also some restrictions maintained for protective purposes. Japan is discriminated against by the U.K., Belgium-Luxembourg, Italy, and the Netherlands: although discrimination by the U.K. and Italy has been significantly reduced over the past couple of years. Hong

Kong is discriminated against by Belgium-Luxembourg and the Netherlands, although in the latter case this does not mean very much. Apart from these cases there is now very little area- or country-discrimination by any of the eight countries; but except for Belgium-Luxembourg, each country has a small list of commodities, mainly primary products, for which quotas or licensing are still in force; (e.g. lead, zinc, and petroleum in the case of the U.S.).

Foreign exchange for *invisible imports* is now freely given, virtually without limit (or, occasionally, within generous limits) provided evidence is given that it *is* required for current transactions, in France, Germany, the Netherlands, the U.S., and the U.K. There are, however, a few restrictions of a protective kind on invisible *transactions* (as opposed to the foreign exchange to finance them) in France and Germany, e.g. on certain insurance, ship-chartering, and film transactions. In Belgium-Luxembourg foreign exchange for gifts, life-insurance payments, remittances by residents or emigrants, inheritances, and private travel expenditure is obtainable freely but must be bought in the 'free' market; i.e. at a rate which may not be quite as favourable as the official rate (but which in practice varies very little from it—see below). Italy is the most restrictive country of the eight on invisible account. There are provisions about insurance, ship-chartering, and films similar to those in Germany; and in addition approval is needed for various other invisible transactions. Tourist travel allowances, where they are still limited at all, are now relatively generous in all eight countries.

Apart from a few regulations imposed for political or military reasons on exports of certain strategic commodities, and exports to the Sino-Soviet bloc (and, in the case of the U.S., to Cuba) *exports* are freely allowed from all countries. Except in Germany, the Netherlands, and the U.S., most foreign exchange earned must normally be

surrendered—i.e. sold at the official rate—to an author-
ized bank. However, all the other countries except the
U.K. have arrangements whereby certain quantities of
foreign exchange earned from exports may be retained in
special accounts. Foreign exchange earned from invisible
transactions is treated similarly, though here it is possible
in the U.K. as well as the other seven countries for institutions operating in the provision of international financial
services to retain balances of foreign exchange.

Briefly, then, the U.K. is virtually as fully liberalized on
current account as the Six and the U.S. Such restrictions
as do exist are supervisory in nature, designed to ensure
that unpermitted capital outflows do not take place under
the guise of current payments.

Capital movements

These are much more complicated. We shall discuss the
Six, the U.K., and the U.S. in turn.

The Common Market countries

Chapter 4 of Title III of the Treaty of Rome (Arts. 67–73)
deals specifically with the liberalization of capital movements envisaged in the Community. The basic principle is
set out in Article 67:

> Member States shall, in the course of the transitional
> period and to the extent necessary for the proper functioning
> of the Common Market, progressively abolish as between
> themselves restrictions on the movement of capital belonging
> to persons resident in Member States and also any discrimin-
> atory treatment based on the nationality or place of residence
> of the parties or on the place in which such capital is invested.

Article 69 states that:

The Council, acting on a proposal of the Commission, which for this purpose shall consult the Monetary Committee . . . shall, in the course of the first two stages by means of unanimous vote and subsequently by means of a qualified majority vote, issue the directives necessary for the progressive implementation of the provisions of Article 67.

There have so far been two such directives: the first was approved by the Council of Ministers in May 1960, the second (which amends and supplements the first) in December 1962. Together, they set a minimum degree of liberalization for the countries of the Common Market. Some of the Six have gone farther than they are required to do. On the other hand, the directives refer only to liberalization as between member countries. Although in most cases liberalization has been extended to countries outside the Common Market this is not always so: where it is not so it is mentioned below.

The first directive grouped capital movements into four lists or categories according to the degree of liberalization which was obligatory. The main effect of the second directive was to abolish the distinction between the first and second lists. Thus there are now three distinct categories.

First category. The most important items in the first category are direct investments and their liquidation and all dealings in quoted stocks and shares across country boundaries. Other items include personal capital flows (i.e. legacies, emigrants' transfer of capital, debt settlements, &c.); short or medium-term credits connected with a commercial transaction in which a resident participates; transfers in implementation of insurance contracts. Movements between EEC countries of all these items have now been liberalized fully, irrevocably, and unconditionally, subject only to temporary recourse in exceptional circumstances to the general escape clauses of the treaty

(Arts. 73, 108, and 109).[1] In most cases the liberalization is by means of an open general licence. In France, individual authorization is normally required, but such administrative controls as do exist are used simply to ensure that the capital flows concerned are for the purposes stated. In Belgium-Luxembourg and the Netherlands foreign exchange for some of these purposes must be obtained on the free market. But the authorities in these countries have undertaken to keep the free rate very close to the official rate.

With the exception of Italy, flows to and from non-EEC countries are equally liberalized. For Italy, direct investment in non-EEC countries must be in the same line of business as that of the Italian firm making the investment and must not exceed the paid-up capital of that firm; and commercial credits to residents of non-EEC countries may not exceed one year. On the other hand personal capital flows to non-member countries may be made freely.

Second category. The most important items in the second category of capital movements are: new issues by foreign enterprises on domestic capital markets; domestic new issues on foreign capital markets; medium-and-long-term credits of a purely financial nature; and transactions in unquoted securities. The directives call for these items to be liberalized conditionally; i.e. restrictions can be retained or reimposed when economic circumstances warrant it (although the Commission has to be consulted and may in fact advise the country concerned to abolish the restriction).

Germany and Belgium-Luxembourg have completely liberalized these movements by open general licence (though in the latter case the 'free' market must be used). France, Italy, and the Netherlands still retrain restrictions

[1] For a discussion of the escape-clause procedure and when it can be adopted see pp. 76–77.

but in practice have acted fairly liberally. The Netherlands have permitted a number of new foreign issues in the past two years, and Italy has allowed both the World Bank and the European Investment Bank to make new issues on its market.

Third category. The third and last category comprises short-term capital movements, the opening of and payments into bank accounts, &c. The directives make no recommendation or stipulation concerning these. In fact such transactions are completely liberalized in Belgium-Luxembourg (through the 'free' market); and liberalized in Germany with the exception that domestic money-market paper (e.g. Treasury bills) may not be sold by residents to non-residents without a licence. In France, the Netherlands, and Italy, although most of these transactions may be carried out by non-residents on the basis of an open general licence, residents are in general restricted from taking part in them.

The United Kingdom

How does the U.K. compare with the Six? First, there is the question of discrimination. In the Six, as we have seen, there is relatively little discrimination in favour of other EEC countries; or at least little in principle: it may be that in cases where individual licences must be granted there is rather more discrimination in practice. There is considerable discrimination by individual countries in favour of their own currency areas relative to the non-EEC world, but I have not thought it worth while for the present purpose to go into this. (The details are easily available in the IMF *Annual Report on Exchange Conditions*.) With the U.K., however, currency-area discrimination is very important. There is virtually no exchange control over dealings with the rest of the sterling area. (The main exceptions occur in payments to Hong Kong.) There is also some measure of freedom in capital transactions with Denmark, Norway, and Sweden. With the exception of these two areas, virtually all capital movements between the U.K. and the rest of the world are controlled in one way or another. The means and effective tightness of the controls, however, vary considerably.

Restriction is by either or both direct control and price. Thus while many transactions may be carried out at the official rate provided permission is obtained (but for many of these transactions permission is difficult or virtually impossible to get), for other movements permission may be more freely or automatically granted provided a 'free' rate of exchange is used. There are two important 'free' exchange markets—broadly one for non-residents and one for residents—security sterling and security 'dollars'. It may be worth-while very briefly outlining the position with regard to each of these.

Security sterling comprises funds held in blocked accounts, which derive from the sale or liquidation of most kinds of U.K. assets by non-residents. Transfers between such blocked accounts are freely permitted and any holdings of security sterling may be sold on the free market for convertible foreign exchange. Like the Belgian and Dutch free rates, the security sterling rate has not in recent years diverged very far from the official rate: in the past three years it has never been more than about $1\frac{1}{2}$ per cent below the official rate; and since the beginning of 1962 has not been more than about $\frac{1}{2}$ per cent below. However, *unlike* the Belgian and Dutch authorities, the U.K. authorities have given no undertaking of any kind to prevent any noteworthy or lasting divergence between the two rates.

Security 'dollars'[2] are analogous to security sterling but in the other direction. They are funds of foreign currency

[2] Sometimes called 'investment dollars' or 'switch dollars'.

(not necessarily dollars) held by U.K. residents and deriving from the sales of foreign securities by residents to non-residents. They are available for the purchase of foreign securities or, in certain cases, for direct investment abroad (see below). Until May 1962, when they were merged, there were two kinds of security 'dollars': the so-called 'hard dollars' which derived from and could only be used for the purchase of U.S. and Canadian dollar securities; and the so-called 'soft dollars' which derived from and could only be used for the purchase of other foreign securities. The security dollar market is altogether much less orderly and predictable than the security sterling market. There is a relatively fixed though large supply (one estimate of the size of the pool when the hard and soft dollar markets were merged was $3,000 million)[3] while demand fluctuates considerably. In the spring of 1961 when sterling was under severe pressure and there was a lot of interest in European securities the premium for 'soft' dollars (the supply of which was relatively small) reached 8 per cent. It fairly soon fell back to around 2–3 per cent where it remained until the 'hard' and 'soft' dollars were merged in May 1962. This merger widened the potential uses of security dollars (see p. 70) and after some months the premium on them began to rise until by the spring and summer of 1963 it was consistently in the region of 7–10 per cent.

There are some other minor markets derived similarly from the application of the principle that foreign exchange derived from the sale of a foreign asset by a U.K. resident may be freely sold to other U.K. residents for the ultimate purpose of buying a similar foreign asset. Thus there is the pool of 'property dollars' derived from the sale by residents of houses or land abroad which are the only means by which residents can buy real estate abroad. The pool of

[3] See *The Times*, 18 May 1962.

property dollars is small and the market is very thin. As a result the rate varies a good deal, often showing a substantial premium.[4]

Now we may discuss U.K. exchange control for the various categories of capital flow.

Direct investment. Direct investment in the non-sterling world by U.K. residents can be undertaken at the official rate only if it can be shown to yield 'commensurate benefits to the balance of payments even in the short run' —a pretty stiff test for almost any kind of direct investment, one would imagine. On satisfying much less stringent criteria, direct investment is now (since May 1962) allowed, by way of the security or investment dollar market. This liberalization has been largely responsible for the increase that we have already noted in the premium on security dollars to 10 per cent or more. Alternatively the investment may be allowed if the enterprise concerned can arrange for the money to be raised by suitable long-term borrowing abroad.

Direct investment in the U.K. by non-residents is fairly freely permitted as long as they provide convertible exchange; but liquidation and repatriation of such capital at the official rate is closely restricted. There are certain projects in which capital directly invested by any non-resident after January 1950 may be repatriated at any time: but there is not a very wide range of these. Residents of Denmark, Norway, and Sweden may repatriate capital freely. With these exceptions, however, the direct repatriation of capital (as opposed to the remittance of profits, dividends, and interest payments which, as current transactions, are unrestricted) is not permitted at the official rate. Any repayment or liquidation of non-resident-owned capital must be credited to a blocked account and repatriated, if desired, through the security sterling

[4] See *The Times*, 13 Sept. 1962.

market. In practice, as we have seen, this has implied a cost of only about ½ per cent for the past year or two; but the security sterling rate is not guaranteed by the authorities.

Investment in real estate abroad by U.K. residents is very tightly controlled as far as the official rate is concerned: official foreign exchange is only granted for such purposes in exceptional circumstances. But, as pointed out above, there is a 'property dollar' market of sorts. If one is able to find a seller of property dollars and willing to pay the premium, one may spend the exchange on buying real estate abroad.

Movements of personal capital. The foreign exchange involved in transferring gifts, legacies, &c. out of the country has to be applied for in all cases. Applications are treated quite liberally, and where the amount is small, approval is virtually automatic.

Dealings in quoted securities. Non-residents may buy quoted British securities with any convertible currency, with external account sterling (i.e. sterling derived from any current transaction) or, if there is no contractual redemption date within five years of the purchase date and they are not optionally payable in foreign currency, with security sterling. Even if sterling securities are bought by a non-resident with convertible foreign exchange, he may only obtain security sterling for them if he sells them. Residents may buy quoted foreign securities but only with security dollars or, on obtaining permission, with any foreign currency capital receipts.

Issue and placing of a domestic enterprise on a foreign capital market. Permission has to be obtained for this, but it has recently (since May 1962) been granted fairly freely. It might well be the 'suitable borrowing' which, if it can be arranged, permits direct investment to be made abroad without passing the very severe test required before official foreign exchange is forthcoming (see above). There have been a number of new issues in Amsterdam and Zurich recently.

Issue and placing of a foreign enterprise on the U.K. capital market. Apart from bond issues by international institutions (e.g. the International Bank) and several sterling-area countries, there had been no foreign new issues in London since the war until 1963. The situation changed rapidly during 1963, however. There were a number of issues denominated in foreign currencies and an enormously successful Japanese loan in sterling. Present trends, which are discussed further below, suggest that there may be more of such issues.

Dealings in unquoted securities abroad. These are virtually forbidden to British residents. The point of making a distinction between public (i.e. quoted) and private (i.e. unquoted) companies abroad is that it would presumably be a relatively simple matter for anyone to set up a private company abroad through which, at the security-dollar rate, he could export capital for whatever purpose he wished. However, British companies may take a minority stake in a private company abroad which is engaged in the same line of business as their own.

Short-term capital transactions. Non-residents may invest in U.K. Treasury bills and other money-market paper, and may open, close, and operate both current and deposit accounts, provided they offer convertible foreign exchange or external-account sterling. None of these operations is permitted in an outward direction.

The United States

Until mid-1963 the only thing to say about U.S. control over capital movements was that there wasn't any. A purist might still say this; but now we have the proposed new interest-equalization tax on U.S. long-term capital outflow. Under the new regulations (if and when they become law), when an American resident purchases a new or outstanding foreign security—either an equity or a long-term bond—he will have to pay a tax. The tax-rate ranges from $2\frac{3}{4}$ per cent on bonds with three years to maturity to a maximum of 15 per cent on equities and bonds with maturity dates longer than $28\frac{1}{2}$ years. The effect of this graduated tax is to raise the interest cost of all foreign long-term borrowing from the U.S.—whether by fixed-interest securities or by equities, and whatever the maturity date—by about 1 per cent. The tax is only paid when an American resident purchases a foreign security from a foreigner; *not* when he buys from another American resident; and not, of course, when a foreigner buys either a foreign or an American security from an American.

This is strictly not exchange control. No official administrative machinery of control has been set up. As President Kennedy said in announcing the tax proposal, 'Under this alternative, the allocation of savings for investment in securities will continue to be the result of decisions based on market prices. There will be no limitations on the marketing of foreign issues and no governmental screening of borrowers.'[5]

However, this is a historic intervention by the U.S. authorities into the field of international capital flows; and its effects will be indistinguishable from certain forms of exchange control. Indeed, it has been pointed out[6] that it will be in one way more restrictive on the U.S. investor than is the security sterling system for the British investor (so long as the security-sterling discount remains at current low levels). A British investor owning a foreign security may switch to another foreign security either at home or abroad with equal ease, while a similar American

[5] USIS Release, 19 July 1963.   [6] *The Times*, 27 July 1963.

investor will be confined unless he pays tax to switching to
a security already held in the U.S.

The U.S. tax will not apply to direct investment, to
obligations with less than three years to run, or to bank
loans. Securities of most underveloped countries are ex-
cluded—though Hong Kong and Japan are included—
and some special arrangements have been made for
Canada.

Comparisons and comments

Current transactions

There is little to choose between the U.K., the Six, and
the U.S. as far as exchange restrictions on current transaction and payments are concerned. All countries have
some protective restrictions: but these pale beside the
restrictions and discriminations in their tariff systems.
Further liberalization on current account must for all
countries mean reductions and removals of discrimination
in tariffs, a subject that falls outside the bounds of this
study.

What about a movement in the other direction: i.e. the
imposition of substantial restrictions on imports as a
measure to protect or improve the balance of payments?
In the case of the U.S. this looks, to put it mildly, very
unlikely. The spirit of the Common Market is against such
a move as between member countries; but it is by no means
unthinkable towards non-member countries. Article 108
of the Rome Treaty, dealing with the position when a
member country is in serious balance-of-payments difficulties, specifically envisages the possibility that the
country 'maintains or re-establishes quantitative restrictions with regard to third countries'. Should the U.K.

resort to import restriction on any such scale to protect her balance of payments?

Perhaps the strongest case for import controls is in a situation like the following. Consumer demand for manufactured goods is rising very fast and outpacing the expansion of capacity to produce them; as a result there is an upsurge of imports causing a balance-of-payments crisis and a restriction of demand; by the time demand has cooled off the extra capacity to produce the goods has been installed only to lie idle. Something very like this happened in 1960. Had consumers been forced to postpone their purchases of durables for six months or so, the argument runs, had they been *prevented* from buying foreign goods, they would then have been able to buy all they wanted from U.K. factories and there would have been no balance-of-payments crisis.

One reply to this argument is that it assumes away the possibility that people might *prefer* foreign goods: if they did, you would have to keep control on indefinitely, and if you did this there would be a loss of welfare and an encouragement of inefficiency. To this it might be reasonably retorted that this limited sacrifice of consumers' sovereignty and of the benefits its discipline entails might be a price worth paying if it enabled the economy to grow faster without being limited by the balance of payments. It does seem to me, however, that import controls would have to be maintained more or less indefinitely if one was not simply to rephase imports in a way we have already discussed (p. 30); but most of the protagonists of import controls do not seem to envisage their semi-permanent retention. Moreover, in these circumstances one would run into serious retaliation problems.

A very important practical consideration is that the machinery for import control has now been abolished. It is one thing to urge, as Sir Roy Harrod has repeatedly

F

done, that controls should not have been dismantled when they were (though in fact I should disagree with him here: in the light of developments in the U.S. balance of payments after 1958 I do not think the U.K. could or should have retained her controls); it is another to urge that controls be reinstated. If one decided to do so in a crisis, matters might well have come to a head before they could be implemented, unless one was prepared to frustrate contracts already entered into in a way which might give a serious long-term blow to Britain's trade. The machinery would have to be set up ahead of any crisis—in which case it might help precipitate one—and at that time administrative energies would be better directed to more constructive long-term solutions of the balance-of-payments problem.

Capital movements

We have seen that liberalization of long-term capital flows has gone a long way within the EEC and that for most of the important flows it is now 'irrevocable': i.e. control can only be reimposed temporarily and in an emergency. Is this likely to be a serious possibility? The conditions are laid down in Article 109 of the Treaty of Rome—the so-called 'escape clause'. This states that a member country 'may provisionally take the necessary measures of safeguard' (which may include control of capital movements) in a sudden crisis, and before a decision on its situation has been taken by the Common Market Commission. Normally, however, the Commission will make its own recommendations in good time; (these may include the granting of 'mutual assistance', i.e. short-term balance-of-payments support by the other member nations). Moreover, if a member country does act under the escape clause, the Council of the EEC may decide by a qualified majority that it must amend, suspend, or abolish any of the measures of safeguard it took.

It is difficult to guess how often this escape-clause procedure will be invoked, because since the inception of the Community the only balance-of-payments problems member countries have had to face have been *embarrasses de richesse*. However, the 'irrevocable' liberalization and the escape-clause procedure relate only to members of the Six. The attitude of the French towards the *inflow* of U.S. direct investment capital, although not shared by other members of the Community, and not likely in the near future to lead to positive restrictions, suggests that at least some of the Six might very well be prepared to discriminate against non-member countries. At present, of course, the problems posed by European restrictions on the outflow of long-term capital to the U.K. or the U.S. are entirely academic. The flows are all in the opposite direction; but future developments might change this.

The U.S., having been totally liberalized on capital account since the war, has now, as we have seen, taken what could be called a half-step towards exchange control on certain particular transactions. It may be that plugging loopholes in the interest-equalization tax will take them a good deal nearer real administrative control. However, this would still represent a very small degree of restriction compared with the U.K.; and further major steps in this direction are unlikely.

The U.K. has herself been liberalizing her control over capital movements quite rapidly in recent years, even if the position so far reached remains legally in terms of regulations much more restrictive than in the U.S. and the Six. As we have seen, many transactions not permitted at the official rate may take place at the security-sterling rate; and at present this involves little cost. After steadily narrowing in the later 1950s, the discount on security sterling has long been as small as that of the Belgian or Dutch 'free rate' discounts. While the security-dollar premium has risen to high levels, this is at least in part due to the fact that outward investment in the non-sterling area has been more liberally permitted through this route.

There is more to capital flows than tightness or looseness of administrative controls; and the influence of Lord Cromer, Governor of the Bank of England, who wants very much to restore London to its one-time eminence as an international capital market, may be seen in many directions. The costs of borrowing in London may still be high compared with some other centres,[7] but they have been reduced by the reduction in stamp duty. There is at the time of writing a bill before Parliament which, if enacted, will make the purchase and transfer of British securities by foreigners easier and less complicated. There has been a breach in the principle of registration of shares and bonds: the ban on the issue of so-called 'bearer' bonds has been removed.

A striking development in 1963 was the floating of a number of new issues denominated in foreign currency. A Belgian and an Italian loan denominated in U.S. dollars came on to the market in the summer and a loan for Copenhagen denominated in Swiss francs appeared in October. Denomination in a foreign currency does not in itself affect the potential strain on the U.K. balance of payments of the debt incurred: that depends on whether the funds come from domestic or foreign saving (see below). It may make a loan more attractive to lenders in so far as they regard the currency concerned as a less serious exchange risk than sterling—and this was the main point of the Swiss franc loan. There is talk from time to time of issuing loans denominated entirely in European units of

[7] See the article on international investment in the *Bank of England Quarterly Bulletin* for June 1963.

account, so as to enable lenders to hedge more completely against the risk of devaluation by any single country. In the case of the U.S. dollar loans the attraction was not so much a smaller exchange risk (which many would not have considered it to be) but that it offered a use for some of the very large eurodollar balances held in London.[8]

Another milestone in 1963 was the floating in August of the first sterling-denominated non-sterling-area loan in London since the war: a £5-million Japanese bond. This was not quite the new development that it sounds because although it was not strictly a conversion issue, it was pretty close to one: most of the proceeds were to be used to redeem some maturing very long-term Japanese bonds, which could themselves be used in payment for subscriptions to the new loan; and conversion issues have in the past not been subject to the same degree of restruction as new issues. However, it is clear that Lord Cromer is moving forward, little by little and on many fronts, as fast as the balance of payments and the Treasury will allow. No doubt he was heartened by the fact that the Japanese loan was twenty-four times over-subscribed. Should he go farther?

Future policy

It is useful to distinguish two types of capital outflow: one that draws on domestic savings and one that draws on foreigners' savings. An increase in the former is obviously likely, *ceteris paribus*, to increase the burden on the balance of payments—though, as we have already seen, the true burden may be smaller than the outflow. Moreover, it may take place at the expense of domestic investment and hence *perhaps* militate against growth. On

[8] For a useful account of the markets in eurocurrencies see two articles by Oscar Altman in *IMF Staff Papers*, viii (1960–1) and x (1963–4).

the other hand, in so far as an outflow, nominally from London (arranged in London by British merchant bankers, for example) is in fact financed from abroad, there may be little burden on the U.K. balance of payments. In the extreme case where say a Swiss bank subscribes to a Japanese issue floated in London (as some did in August 1963) there will be no burden at all: indeed there will be a net gain from the commission earned by the underwriters. If the inflows of capital are kept equal to the outflows, but not precisely related to them as in the previous example, the net effect on the balance should consist of the gain from the City's earnings and the difference (positive or negative) between the interest paid on funds borrowed and that received on funds lent. However, if the funds borrowed are genuinely more liquid or volatile than those lent, the vulnerability of the balance of payments will have increased. We have already noted that it is extremely difficult to classify different elements in the balance of payments in terms of their volatility; but this is, of course, not to deny that some funds *are* more volatile than others and that therefore some positions are more vulnerable than others.

Lord Cromer is keen to develop at least the second kind of capital outflow—that financed by corresponding inflows; what he has called an entrepôt trade in capital. There are obvious possibilities in this because of the backwardness of most of the Continental capital markets. For the past few years we have witnessed the ridiculous sight of the Common Market countries, which were all rapidly increasing their reserves, borrowing heavily from the U.S. which was rapidly losing reserves.

One of the reasons for this has been the low relative level of interest rates in the U.S. In the first half of 1963, for example, U.S. long-term government-bond yields were some 2 per cent below comparable yields in Germany,

1½ per cent below the U.K., and 1 per cent below France and Italy. Plagued by high unemployment and slow growth, the U.S. authorities were for long understandably reluctant to raise their rates. However, they were unsuccessful in persuading the Europeans to lower their rates sufficiently to affect the flow, and therefore in 1963 they began to let their own rates rise and proposed the interest-equalization tax which may be thought of as an ingenious device for raising external rates without raising those affecting the domestic economy.

These moves are, however, unlikely fully to remedy the position because there remains the second main reason for the one-way flow across the Atlantic—the inadequacy of the European capital markets.[9] Despite the vaunted liberalization of EEC capital movements, relatively little foreign borrowing has occurred in any of the Continental markets apart from Amsterdam and Zurich (and the capacity of these centres has been very limited). The problem is that even domestic borrowing is often difficult in Paris or Frankfurt. There are incomparably fewer channels for funds than in New York or London in these centres where self-finance and bank finance have traditionally dominated the scene; and where monetary institutions and mechanisms are frequently very primitive.

The U.S. authorities have been urging in the strongest terms that these markets be developed. So have the EEC and the OECD. So finally, and no doubt most effectively, have the voices of nationalism. In June 1963, for example, the Lorain Report (roughly analogous to our Radcliffe Report) was published in France. It made many recommendations for improving French financial and capital markets. Both the authorities and private institutions in

---

[9] See the article already referred to in the *Bank of England Quarterly Bulletin*, June 1963; and Peter Kenen, 'Towards an Atlantic Capital Market', *Lloyds Bank Review*, July 1963.

France appear at present to be making a strong bid to make Paris the leading financial centre of the Community.

In the face of these developments what should the U.K. do? The Bank and the City argue that if she opens her markets now she is assured of primacy among the financial centres of Europe, and that the consequent earnings will make a significant contribution to the balance of payments; if on the other hand she maintains her post-war policy of restriction, she is likely to find in a few years that the Continental centres have stolen a march on her, establishing a position which she will then find difficult or impossible to challenge.

Against this one may argue that it is more convincing on the demand than the supply side: it is easy to envisage queues of French and German borrowers coming to London instead of New York if the interest rates, &c. were right; but what about the lenders? There have been no floods of Europeans with funds to lend in New York recently. If there had been, the U.S. problem would have been greatly eased. There might have been no need for the interest-equalization tax or for the artificial way in which the U.S. authorities have had to arrange that the outflows were financed—by putting strong pressure on the Continental monetary authorities to lend to the U.S. in the form both of advance repayment of debt and of holding dollar balances rather than converting them into gold.

It may have been partly that U.S. interest rates were too low; but if London rates are to be high enough to attract foreign lenders, it may be difficult to make a net profit out of the borrowers. Too much should not be made of this since the strength of the London market is that by virtue of its many channels it is likely to be able to offer a wide range of borrowers exactly the kind of asset that they want.

However, the fact remains that the potential lenders are probably less in evidence than the potential borrowers.

More important, as their own capital markets develop they are likely increasingly to find what they want at home. Further, as we have seen, the authorities in the Six may restrict outflows even of long-term capital, much more of short-term capital, to non-member countries when they are individually in difficulties. Funds from these countries will have a potential volatility over and above interest rate and confidence movements.

Two further, somewhat different, points may be made. First, such outflows of long-term capital as the U.K. can foster or afford should surely be directed as far as possible to underdeveloped countries. Our emphasis in development aid is, rightly in my view, on government loans and grants. But doubtless private capital also has a role in financing development. At present our exchange restrictions do not very strongly work towards this end: investment in the sterling area is unrestricted but the bulk of it goes to the rich members (Australia and New Zealand) or the semi-developed such as the Rhodesias. If we could mobilize some Continental savings for investment in underdeveloped areas this might be a justification for reducing our restrictions further. But the likelihood is that the bulk of such new flows as we stimulated would stay in the relatively developed areas of the world—especially Europe.

Secondly, we must be careful to distinguish the hard cash that our financial institutions can earn us in the world from the cloudier glories of being Top Financial Centre. Much of the justly famed city expertise can be and is being put to work without the removal of exchange control. The merchant banks in particular have been very active in Europe's capital markets in the last couple of years. Most of them have formed investment trusts operating in European securities; and they are increasingly often involved in European financing operations jointly with Continental houses. The institutions providing financial services—the insurance companies, the banks, &c.—provide the bulk of the City's foreign earnings in their current transactions which are not subject to restriction at all.

There remains the larger, vaguer question of facing Europe or turning one's back on it; or indeed of helping or hindering international monetary co-operation. I believe we should not 'turn our back on Europe'; we should try to do things which work in the ultimate direction of union with Europe and avoid doing things which do not; and I certainly believe we should do everything possible to foster international monetary co-operation. But I do not believe that these aims require further major dismantling of our exchange controls. These controls are permitted under our IMF agreement and are unlikely seriously to provoke retaliation.

To the extent, however, that their dismantlement could be used as a bargaining counter (even if not completely explicitly) towards stronger guarantees from other countries of balance-of-payments assistance, there would be much to be said for it. Were the question of joining the Common Market an issue at the moment, I should myself not boggle too greatly at the liberalization of capital movements which would be involved, because it would be part of a major and important collaboration. After all, perhaps the main fact about the U.K. balance of payments is that it is already—and has been since the war—so vulnerable that if the skies get really stormy sterling can always be brought down unless official help is forthcoming. Thus the most important aim must be to strengthen the framework of official help: in relation to this, particular increases in the potential volatility of a particular part of the balance of payments are of smaller importance. It is to sterling's place in the international monetary framework that we now turn.

7

Sterling as a Key Currency[1]

As the Brussels negotiations moved towards a climax there was much talk in financial circles about the possibilities for world liquidity that would be opened up if the U.K. joined the Common Market. 'Sterling can become the currency of Europe', it was said; or 'A perfect marriage can be arranged—between EEC assets and U.K. liabilities'. Not surprisingly, most of the people who spoke in this way were British—though there were some transatlantic matchmakers too. On the Continent even those who were most enthusiastic to have Britain join were noticeably reticent on this particular subject. But whatever the possibilities really were, the marriage is now off. Left at the altar by his prospective bride with the beautiful dowry, sterling has already seen some of his fairweather friends slip quickly away. As we have seen, he has been approached by sophisticated stag-party associates who suggest that he should immediately cheapen himself or even consciously abandon himself to a career of perpetual dissipation. On the other side are voices urging him to stay pure against the day when his bride changes his mind again. More realistic counsels speak of the adult attractions of passing or semi-permanent liaisons. Finally (but here the metaphor must undoubtedly be discontinued before it becomes too unpersuasive) it is suggested in some quarters that a new approach be made towards a multilateral solution of the problems that

[1] A somewhat different version of this chapter was published in the *Journal of Common Market Studies*, ii/1.

derive from sterling's role as a key currency. What are these problems? What should be done about them?

Two paradoxes

Much has been written on the shortcomings and potential shortcomings of the key-currency system as a whole, and I do not propose seriously to add to it; but a few general remarks are perhaps worth making. At present virtually all the world's official reserves consist of gold, dollars, or sterling. At the end of 1962 total holdings amounted to some $58 billion, of which $67\frac{1}{2}$ per cent was gold, 21 per cent dollars, and $11\frac{1}{2}$ per cent sterling. Seven years earlier the total had been $49 billion and the corresponding proportions 71, $13\frac{1}{2}$, and $15\frac{1}{2}$ per cent. Of the increase of $9 billion, about $4 billion had come from gold and $5\frac{1}{2}$ billion from dollars; sterling holdings had actually declined somewhat.

Professor Triffin has pointed out[2] one intrinsic source of weakness in a situation whereby much of the world's additional demand for liquidity is provided for by an increase in sterling or dollar liabilities: these can normally increase only as a result of overall deficits in the U.K. or U.S. balances of payments; and these deficits themselves tend to bring the currencies under suspicion. Thus the more liquidity is provided in this way the worse it becomes —the less willingly will people hold it in bad times. Whether one regards this in practice, or right now, as a serious weakness in the system depends on one's views about the adequacy of the present volume of liquidity for the next five or ten years, and on the ways in which the system can be tinkered with, patched up, assisted by the IMF, and so on. But it would be hard to deny that this is an inherent *potential* weakness.

[2] On a number of occasions, but most recently in an article in *The Banker*, Aug. 1963.

There is another, related paradox in the running of a reserve currency. The authorities responsible for running a reserve currency normally believe that just because it *is* a reserve currency, because of the existence of the outstanding balances, they cannot afford to devalue it. They may be right or wrong in this (for the reasons discussed in Section 5, I think they are right), but they do think it. They do not regard an alteration in the exchange rate as a genuine alternative to other policies for correcting a disequilibrium in the balance of payments. But some people are not convinced of this at all; and when the balance of payments looks in bad shape—or likely to hinder domestic expansion—they are apt to recommend adjusting the exchange rate: e.g. in the correspondence columns of *The Times* last March or in the *National Institute Economic Review passim*. Certainly many of the people who *hold* the currency believe that there is a genuine chance that it will be devalued; and the effects of this may be seen, for example, in the movements to get out of sterling in 1957 and 1961 and to get out of dollars in 1960. This is surely an intolerable situation. It must be in the interests of both the U.S. and the U.K. to find some way out of it.

From the way in which the position is put it is clear that there are two possible directions of escape. Either the holders of the currency must be convinced once and for all that it will never be devalued; or the country must get out of the business of running a reserve currency so that the real as opposed to the nominal possibility of devaluation is restored to it. The former solution obviously leaves the country concerned with less freedom of action than does the latter: but, if it were really achieved, it would represent a great improvement over the existing position in that fluctuations in other elements in the balance of payments would no longer be exaggerated by leads and lags and confidence-inspired flows of short-term capital.

One might expect that on these questions the interests of the U.S. and the U.K.—the two reserve currency providers—would be similar; and that it would suit them both to work, however slowly, towards a multilateral solution of all the liquidity problems—that is, towards a situation where the world's liquidity was provided by a multilateral arrangement—so that ultimately full freedom of action was restored to both of them; and that the framework within which they would prefer to work would be the IMF—especially since their combined voting strength in that institution is some 40 per cent of the total.

U.S. and U.K. policies

The U.K. authorities have indeed been working in this direction. For some years they have been exploring ways of increasing the Fund's potentialities and were, for example, very strongly in favour of the increase in quotas in 1959 and of an increase in effective lending power in 1961. Admittedly they have not come out in favour of the Triffin Plan or anything like it: but perhaps this is not an infallible test of multilateralist virtue. Moreover, the scheme put forward for consideration at the annual meeting of the IMF in September 1962 by Mr Maudling would represent, whatever its merits or demerits, a significant move towards the multilateralizing of liquidity arrangements if it were implemented.[3] If the Americans were prepared to co-operate, I think the U.K. authorities would probably go a long way in schemes to strengthen and widen the IMF's role. But it is admittedly hard to say just how far they would go, since the Americans have, until very recently, shown themselves decidedly unwilling to co-operate.

American coolness towards the Maudling proposals in

[3] The 'Maudling Plan' is discussed below (see pp. 102–3).

Washington in September 1962 was widely noted. But as a snub this was mild compared with that implied in an article by Mr Roosa, Under-Secretary of the U.S. Treasury, which had appeared a few days earlier.[4] In over 5,000 words on the subject of providing and assuring international liquidity for the world, he did not mention sterling once. The U.S. is constantly referred to either directly or by implication as the only provider of liquidity for the world, and at one point he says: 'Dollars are still the currency towards which all countries turn for a substantial part, if not the entire amount, of their international payments.' So much for the sterling area: so much for ten years' work by the Information Division of Her Majesty's Treasury, inserting into countless official speeches and documents the proud claim that 'over 40 per cent of the world's trade is conducted in sterling'. Here, surely, was a snub on the grand scale; and, like all snubs, deeper and more truly wounding if it was not deliberate.

Mr Roosa was clearly going to have nothing to do with any joint U.S.–U.K. approaches towards a multilateral solution. His solution was fundamentally and explicitly bilateral (it represents in fact a well worked out version of the second possible way out of the reserve currency country's dilemma referred to above, and set out and discussed below, pp. 98–99). There are no doubt many reasons for his disregard of sterling (one good one, it is salutary to remind ourselves, is that as we have seen, sterling has not provided any *new* liquidity for many years).[5] But perhaps the most important reason—certainly

---

[4] 'Assuring the Free World Liquidity', *Business Review of the Federal Reserve Bank of Philadelphia*, Sept. 1962.

[5] However, this picture of sterling's role since the war is misleading. Arithmetically, the U.K. added to world reserves during the war and has not done so since, but the war-induced sterling balances were of very limited use to their owners in the immediate post-war period. The movement towards full convertibility of sterling has greatly improved their 'quality' while not increasing their volume.

the most interesting from our present point of view—is suggested by the following sentence (which contains incidentally the only reference to the U.K., as distinct from the London gold market, in the entire article):

At the same time, it is conceivable that work can go forward through . . . the OECD. towards preparing the way for the next stage of practicable and foreseeable innovation in the area of international financial arrangements—the fusing of the United Kingdom into the Common Market; the evolution of a unified financial mechanism to serve the expanded Common Market; and the forging of appropriate operating and policy links between that organization, once it emerges, and our own financial institutions.

As in so many political and commercial issues, so in international monetary policy it is clear that the Americans were bending their efforts towards getting the U.K. into the EEC and basing their policies on the assumption that they would be successful.

But General de Gaulle knocked that plan, like many others, on the head. Early in 1963 it became clear that even if the Common Market countries did ultimately fuse their economic and monetary systems to the extent of creating anything which could be called a common external currency—a europa—there would still be three major currencies in the world, not two. Moreover, it soon began to look as if, perhaps because of the trauma inflicted by the General, the process of integration by the Six was slowing up: the creation of any kind of europa might be long delayed. It was clear that the dollar would have to start talking with sterling; and this indeed it very soon did, getting the conversation off to a cracking start with the $500 million dollar-sterling 'swap' in May. A further consequence was that the Americans were now much more likely to be prepared to think in terms of a multilateral solution to the world's liquidity problems, in the context of the IMF; and sure enough in July came the announcement that the U.S. was negotiating a stand-by credit of $500 million with the IMF for the first time since that institution was set up. At the same time President Kennedy spoke about the possibilities of reforming international liquidity arrangements in a way which, though still quite unspecific, suggested that the U.S. authorities were prepared to look more favourably at new multilateral 'plans' than they had done in the past.

Two possible lines of development for sterling, and liquidity generally, are outlined below: first, a 'bilateral' approach, aimed ultimately at totally protecting the existing key currencies by bringing other currencies individually to perform some of the functions of key currencies; and secondly, a 'multilateral' approach, aimed ultimately at replacing all national key currencies by an international currency. The two approaches are not mutually exclusive, however, and could in fact lead to somewhat the same results.

Take the 'bilateral' approach first. Can the U.S. and the U.K. convince the holders of dollars and sterling that they will never devalue by choice and never be put into the position where they are forced to devalue? One paradoxical way of going about this would be for them to engineer an immediate world devaluation: i.e. raise the price of gold. This is really a matter for U.S. policy and perhaps does not strictly concern us in a study of possible U.K. policies, but it must be discussed, however briefly, because of its bearing on all the alternatives.

Revaluing gold

Raising the price of gold is repeatedly urged not merely by the government of South Africa but by a number of independent commentators—among whom 'Lombard' in the *Financial Times* and Sir Roy Harrod are notable for the persistence of their advocacy. The basic argument can be simply stated: the world is short of reserves (or will be) and the process of supplementing the growth in gold reserves by a growth in currency reserves is increasingly unsatisfactory; why not then, say, double the world's gold reserves by the stroke of a pen? All that is necessary is that the U.S. should announce that in future it will buy and sell gold not at $35 an ounce but at, say, $70. By this means, there would be ample liquidity for a long time to come.

This solution is certainly simple, but in my view that is about all that can be said for it. First, it is terribly clumsy. If the revaluation is to mean that there will be enough liquidity in fifteen or twenty years' time it will mean that the price has to be raised so far that there is too much liquidity now; i.e. substantial inflationary pressure will be generated. Moreover, the distribution of the gains would be haphazard or worse. I am not so much worried by the fact that Russia and South Africa would do particularly well; for after all the main gains would accrue to the U.S. and the U.K., the key-currency countries. But what about the people who are holding (and in many cases have been persuaded, somewhat against their will, to hold) these key currencies? Doubling the price of gold at the end of 1962 would have raised France's reserves by 43 per cent, but Germany's by only 15 per cent because Germany was holding more of the obligations of the country which raised the gold price. Surely the most likely outcome in the years following a gold revaluation would be a major flight from both key currencies into gold, so as never to be caught again. This destruction of liquidity would go a long way to offset the original increase. And from now on all external-transactions balances would be more volatile than ever. The argument that the U.S. and the U.K. would now have so much stronger backing for their currencies that they would be safe to hold would be outweighed by the counter-argument that they would have shown that they were prepared to reduce the gold value of their currencies when things got tough, and there would be no reason to expect that they wouldn't do so again.

Guaranteeing the exchange rate

If there is so much to be said against a gold revaluation, perhaps it is not an impossible task for the U.S. and U.K. authorities to convince all holders of their currencies that they will never devalue. One of the main advantages of pursuing this general policy is that it represents simply a further move in the direction in which international monetary policies have been moving in the past three years. It is easy to underestimate the magnitude of the changes that have occurred in international monetary cooperation in this time, as a result partly of the pressure of circumstances, and partly of the pressure of Mr Roosa, who is firmly and explicitly committed to what we have called the 'bilateral' approach. How then, we may ask, can one go about implementing it?

At first sight the simplest way to convince holders of your currency that you are not going to devalue—or, what amounts to the same thing, to prevent their being worried by the possibility that you may—is to guarantee the present gold value of the holdings. In fact both the U.S. and the U.K. have set their faces firmly against doing this. The strongest argument against doing it is probably that if you do not guarantee all holdings you create as many problems as you solve, while if you do guarantee them all, and your cover is insufficient, you will not be believed. After all, as Mr Roosa has pointed out, the United States once abrogated a gold clause in contracts and the action was supported by the Supreme Court and approved by a joint resolution of Congress. The only way one would be likely to hold the confidence of important holders of one's currency (i.e. other central banks) that the guarantee could always be honoured would be by following balance-of-payments policies that they approved. The size of the deficits that were run, the speed with which they were reduced, the liquid asset-liability ratio that was maintained—all these would be dictated at least in part by holders of the currency if they were to accept the guarantee as meaningful: if, that is to say, they were to be prepared to hold more of the currency (and in worse times) with the guarantee than they would have done without it.

For these (in my view strong) reasons the U.S. and the U.K. are opposed to guarantees. Until recently the U.K. accepted the requirements of guarantees for holdings in the European Monetary Agreement. But the authorities were under considerable pressure from the Australians and other sterling-area countries who always resented the discrimination between sterling-holders implied by the guarantee, and in February 1963 the old arrangement came to an end. Only funds held as working balances by central banks—an almost negligible sum—now carry a guarantee.[6]

Bilateral arrangements

Leaving guarantees on one side, one can convince currency-holders of the immutability of the currency they are holding by enlisting support for it whenever it runs into trouble, and by showing that one will always be able to, and will, enlist such support. Support may be drawn both from the IMF and from other countries, of course. But the keynote of American policy in the past two years has been the building up of bilateral arrangements where-

[6] Apart from the 'swaps', discussed immediately below.

by short-term help is given; and, more important, mechanisms are installed, and seen to be installed, which could at a time of serious stress in the future give very substantial support indeed. These are the well-known currency swaps: agreements whereby an individual European country agrees (say) to hold for three months 100 million of dollars while the U.S. holds $100 million of its currency. By late 1963 the Federal Reserve had negotiated currency swaps with ten foreign central banks involving a total of $1,600 million.[7]

These arrangements have what is so far only a relatively minor by-product: while they are in existence they create liquidity. In the example just quoted the reserves of each country rise by $100 million when the swap takes place (giving a total increase in reserves—or liquidity—of $200 million). Of course, if the swap is only for three months, there is a corresponding drop of $200 million in world liquidity at the end of the period. Obviously, however, semi-permanent arrangements of this kind on a large scale might make a significant contribution to the growth of world liquidity. But this is still in the future. So far the effect has been largely one of protecting the dollar against short-term movements by enabling the U.S. authorities to operate in the various foreign-currency markets. There is a close relation of the swap which yields much more substantial help, and this too has been greatly developed: this is the willingness of other central banks to acquire and hold the reserve currency when there is pressure on it, i.e. when private holders are selling it. One can think of this as representing simply a shift in the composition of liabilities instead of a reduction of liabilities and assets *pari passu*—without the deterioration in 'cover' and bad confidence effects that the latter alternative is likely to

[7] $500 million of this was with the U.K. and was technically not a currency swap; but the effect of it was the same (see p. 97 below).

involve. Or one can think of it as the extension of short-term loans by the other countries; or as the acceptance by them of the fact that the reserve currency is not (for official holders) fully convertible. As in all such matters as these, effects are cumulative, and the successful use of both rescue and routine currency-holding operations helps each time to build confidence further.

In addition, the U.S. Treasury has straightforwardly borrowed more than $500 million of foreign currencies in recent months. And finally, there has been the development of the arrangements between central banks to stabilize the London gold market. All these moves are aspects of the overall U.S. policy of persuading individual countries to help support the reserve currencies when they are under pressure.

The U.K., as already mentioned, has been more interested in exploring the possibilities of long-term multilateral solutions than has the U.S. However, in her relationship both with the IMF and with individual countries she has progressed a long way towards effectively establishing that routine or semi-routine support will always be available to the pound. The U.K. has twice gone to the IMF for a large loan in the past six years, and on each occasion has repaid the loan well within the stipulated period. Again, the effects of such measures are cumulative: not merely do the loans immediately improve the balance of payments by reversing the speculative movements, but over time the policy of going easily 'in and out' can come to be seen as semi-routine; the U.K. drawing rights at the IMF come to be regarded as our 'second-line reserves', as the authorities now very properly describe them.

Secondly, there was the so-called Basle arrangement whereby the European central banks in effect lent us over £300 million for three months, early in 1961, and again gave us some help in the spring of 1963.[8] These were very short term, and rescue rather than routine operations; but the important thing is that they happened and happened twice. The Europeans have demonstrated in a practical, even if limited, way their commitment to support sterling.

Until the summer of 1963, however, the U.K. had not gone in very much for bilateral swapping. Nothing more formal and continuing than the Basle arrangements had been undertaken with the Europeans; and there had been only a token three-months' exchange of £18 million for $50 million with the U.S. Then at the end of May came the dramatic development of a U.K.–U.S. 'swap' of $500 million. This did not in fact take the form of an exchange of obligations: the reserves of the two countries were not increased. Each country simply agreed to provide the other with an automatic line of credit up to $500 million; but the effect is the same. This obviously represents a substantial step by the U.K. authorities in the direction of the Roosa approach. It also presumably reflects some of the rethinking necessitated for the Americans by the breakdown at Brussels. It may also be that the U.K. exacted as a price for this swap more U.S. interest in multilateral approaches.

Now what about developing currency swaps with the Europeans? Could we along these lines achieve the monetary 'fusion' of the U.K. and the Common Market of which Mr Roosa spoke in September 1962 (or something like it) even though we shall not be achieving economic or political fusion?

[8] By increasing their official and private holdings of sterling, and undertaking not to convert them into gold for a limited period. In fact the two operations were technically slightly different (see *Bank of England Quarterly Bulletin*, Sept. 1961 and June 1963).

A European currency?

There is a good deal to be said for this approach. It might be possible to develop, over time, long-range 'permanent' exchanges of currencies between the U.K. and the Six themselves. (They might well be short-run in form, but renewed continually in a routine way.) This arrangement would have a number of advantages. It would, as with any swap, increase total liquidity; and this increase would have two important aspects. First, within Europe settlements could be increasingly made out of the liabilities which each country would hold of all the other members. Thus as the system developed there would be less and less need for gold or dollars to move between members. At the same time there would be a ready-made mechanism for the extension of balance-of-payments assistance to any particular country. This assistance could take the form of agreements by the other central banks to allow settlements to be made, for a limited period largely or entirely out of liabilities instead of gold.

The second opportunity provided by this procedure would be in the field of payments with the rest of the world, in particular by the U.K. The sterling balances would be backed by larger reserves—as substantial quantities of marks, francs, &c., were added to the gold and dollars. Of course, sterling liabilities would grow by an exactly equal amount as the authorities in the Six increased their holdings of sterling. But, as has already been pointed out, the 'cover', or the ratio between assets and liabilities, is improved by the addition of an equal sum on both sides. If this increased 'cover' was to mean anything it would, however, have to be available to be drawn on. Thus the Germans, for example, in implementing this 'permanent' swap would have to agree that a certain proportion over a certain period of time could be drawn from our reserves in making normal settlements. In such a case marks would either be held by a creditor of the U.K. or presented to the German authorities who would redeem them with gold.

Such an arrangement would thus mean gradually bringing the European currencies to play in a minor way the role of reserve currencies. There would no doubt to begin with be very strict limitations on the extent to which the authorities of the Six would allow their currencies to be exposed to claims by U.K. creditors; and in so far as they did allow this they would demand a say in the policies being followed by the U.K.—her development aid, the deficits she was running, and so on. This is inescapable. In his article Mr Roosa rejected both a multilateral solution and gold guarantees on the grounds that this would mean a serious loss of sovereignty for the U.S., but in his proposed approach, which if carried far enough would look rather like that which has just been outlined, he has to admit, though in a guarded and inexplicit way—he speaks of 'additional consultation and negotiation'—a loss of sovereignty which could be at least as great as those he dismissed. (There may, of course, be an important reason for his preferring to lose sovereignty in the second way: it may be easier to conceal from, or justify to, Congress.) In any case from our point of view the loss of sovereignty is perhaps less serious: we are already less sovereign than the U.S. and *much* less sovereign than we appear to be.

Whether, even if these arrangements were freely implemented, many marks, francs, &c., would end up in the possession of present holders of sterling balances may be doubted. Some would, perhaps, but in general the fact that U.K. capital and financial markets are so much more developed and varied than those of the Six would probably mean that most balances would continue to be held in sterling. Indeed, there might be a substantial increase in the holdings of sterling as the currencies of the Six were seen to be involved more and more closely in its support. As the exchange risk diminished the advantages of financial return (if short-term interest rates were normally higher in the U.K. for example) and convenience might bring a more or less steady inflow—thus providing some normal support for the U.K.'s balance of payments.

What about the second, 'multilateral' type of solution? There is already a plethora of plans for turning the IMF into a super central bank able to create international money by operations in particular countries, very much as a domestic central bank creates domestic credit by open-market operations. The difficulty with all such plans is that though they are intellectually attractive, and even exciting, and though I for one believe that some such arrangement both should and will ultimately prevail, they presuppose a degree of political supranational agreement which does not yet exist. Creating money is not a technical matter: it is a highly important political activity; and this power cannot be handed over to an international body until there is some kind of political consensus that it is a desirable thing to do.

The Europeans' views

At the moment, there is no such consensus. The Americans may now be coming around to the view that to yield this much sovereignty to the IMF is the right thing to do, and in the U.S.'s own interest, but this remains to be seen: certainly they have been hostile to such schemes hitherto.[9] More important, the Europeans who are in the key position of being the creditor nations at present

[9] At least the Treasury and the Federal Reserve have been: there has been some sympathy in the Council of Economic Advisers.

(or at least those acquiring *liquid* external assets), have been very strongly of the opinion that no radical reforms of the present system are necessary or desirable.

It is no use wishing such views away and there is no excuse for pretending that they do not exist. In its Fourth Report, issued in March 1962, the Monetary Committee of the EEC stated that it approved the conclusions of a working party it had set up to consider the problems of international liquidity: the working party, though considering that various improvements could be made in co-operation between central banks, and admitting that in the long run certain problems of liquidity shortage might emerge, was categorical in its views, (*a*) that the main thing that needed to be done was for the U.S. and the U.K. to remove their deficits on their 'basic' balances of payments; and (*b*) that plans for reforming the IMF such as that put forward by Professor Triffin were not feasible or desirable. The working party, incidentally, dismissed what it called 'proposals of some British authors'—i.e. the suggestions of Messrs Balogh, Day, and Stamp—in the following words:

On the whole the Working Party considers that the suggestions of the various British authors, the technical aspects of which are incidentally in most cases not sufficiently thought out and the majority of which appear to be geared to the U.K. interests, even less realizable than those of Triffin.[10]

Perhaps one can read some change of attitude in the Fifth Report of the Monetary Committee (May 1963) where it is stated that the Committee has examined various proposals for improving the international monetary system, and that it 'intends to pursue actively its consideration of this problem, though for the moment its

[10] EEC. Monetary Committee Working Party for Problems of International Liquidity, *Report on Current Problems of International Liquidity* (Brussels, July 1961). (Eng. trans. by Deutsche Bundesbank.)

studies are still at the theoretical stage'. But no one in any position of responsibility in Europe has come out for any major new multilateral approach—any radical reform of the IMF or other existing institutions.

The Continental position is simply this. They are prepared, as they have shown over the past two or three years, to provide substantial short-term assistance to protect either or both the reserve currencies; but the more such assistance they provide and the longer or more frequently they provide it, the more say they want in how the U.S. and the U.K. handle their balances of payments. Moreover, they are deeply suspicious of any plans which may put the control of the volume of liquidity that is provided in the hands of an institution where the debtor countries—the U.S. and the U.K.—can muster more than 40 per cent of the votes. They believe such schemes are likely (indeed may be designed) to enable the U.S. and the U.K. to avoid putting their houses in order, whereas it is just this rectifying action which they believe is most needed.

If any plan for reforming the IMF is to have the slightest chance of success it must accept these views as a fact—and indeed recognize their force and plausibility. The kind of plan which we must aim at is one which over the passage of time, as the IMF and member countries get used to running it (and perhaps as some of the present creditors turned into debtors), could *evolve into* a credit-creating mechanism; but which in its original form would involve no credit creation and no evasion by the debtor countries of their basic commitments; and would ask no more of the creditor countries than limited short-term assistance such as they have in fact been prepared to provide.

The 'Maudling Plan' represented one such limited suggestion. In essence the proposal was that when countries were accumulating more sterling or dollar balances than they wished to possess, instead of cashing them for gold in the traditional way, or holding them reluctantly in response to the blandishments of Mr Roosa or Lord Cromer, they should deposit them at the IMF in a 'mutual-currency account'. In exchange they would receive a gold-guaranteed credit with the account which would form part of their reserves. This would not be transferable; it would be used only to redeem that country's own currency at such time as it might be in surplus. For example, suppose France runs a surplus of £50 million with the U.K.; the most traditional financing procedure is for her to acquire £50 million in gold from the U.K. More recently, under 'Roosa' and 'Basle' arrangements, she may agree to hold, for some period, a claim on the U.K. without exercising it (i.e. a sterling balance). In these circumstances she gets a confidential gold guarantee. The Maudling Plan may be seen as an institutionalizing and multilateralizing of these arrangements. It could have the advantage that the deposits in the mutual-currency account were longer-lived than the 'temporary' holdings of dollars and sterling. Not until France was in deficit, in our example, and in a position to incur liabilities of £50 million to the U.K., would she redeem her credit with the mutual-currency account and hence liquidate these liabilties.

This seems to me an ingenious and promising approach. (It was put forward simply as a general approach, not as a specific plan worked out in detail.) Perhaps now in the post-Brussels world it will get a more sympathetic hearing from the Americans than it received when it was first put forward. But while it represents in some ways an advance and an improvement on recent American policies, it also has drawbacks which these policies have not—or have in a less pronounced degree. Basically, it opens up the gold-guarantee dilemma already discussed: either you guaran-

tee all holdings, in which case you are not believed, or you
guarantee only certain holdings, in which case you vastly
increase the volatility of the holdings not guaranteed.
Which holders of sterling balances would have the right
to use the mutual-currency account? The original
Maudling suggestion was that it should be restricted to
'major' currency countries—perhaps the members of the
so-called Paris Club;[11] but what about the traditional
holders of sterling—the sterling-area countries? Again,
would one be allowed to convert sterling holdings into
deposits with the mutual-currency account without limit
or only above certain levels? Either alternative carries
serious problems. The 'swap' technique and the *ad hoc*
persuasion of individual countries to hold more sterling or
dollars have the advantage, at least if they are not carried
too far, that two kinds of key currency or two kinds of key-
currency holders—one with a preferential guarantee—are
not *formally* and *explicitly* created.

An alternative, limited, multilateral approach that
might be explored is some version of 'handing over' some
of the sterling balances to the IMF. A number of such
schemes has been put forward[12] many of which involve
giving true liquidity-creating powers to the IMF. I have
suggested that I think it is not possible, or perhaps even
desirable, to do this yet. Are there any schemes which
would stop short of this and yet prove useful?

A limited 'multilateral' proposal

First and simplest, the IMF could take over some or all
of the dollar and sterling liabilities in exchange for long-

[11] Belgium, Canada, France, Germany, Italy, Japan, Netherlands,
Sweden, U.K., and U.S.
[12] See, for example, Mr A. C. L. Day's evidence to the Radcliffe Committee.

term credits with the U.S. and the U.K. Thus the balances would be funded as far as the debtors (the U.S. and the U.K.) were concerned, but would remain liquid as far as the creditors were concerned, being backed (in ways to be discussed in a moment) by the IMF. A solution along these lines would have the attraction for the U.K. that her debt-repayment burden was fixed and known; speculative movements would no longer dictate her policies and she would be free to devalue if she wished. However, unless the credit were *very* long-term the annual burden would be very heavy. Moreover, repayment of all the balances might be inappropriate. It would have a substantial deflationary effect over the years, representing a continuous destruction of liquidity (on the assumption that the IMF were not creating any new liquidity).

A more attractive variant of this scheme would be to hand the liabilities over to the IMF in exchange for a perpetual, non-redeemable debt. Interest would be payable by the U.K. to the IMF which would in turn pay interest to the one-time sterling holders who now held a new type of IMF obligation. This would obviously involve no new burden on the U.K. and would indeed be very attractive to her. In fact it would be very nice for everyone, if from the moment when the transfer was made no one holding one of the new IMF obligations (let us call them IMF-sterling) wanted to increase or reduce his holdings.

However, the whole point of holding liquid reserves is that you can increase or reduce them at will. It would be necessary to devise a scheme whereby short-term rises and falls in holdings of IMF-sterling were prevented from dislocating the U.K. balance of payments, but longer-term movements had their full effect. In other words, one might ask creditor countries collectively for short-term credit (as they have been asked individually in the past few years) but one would not ask them to 'underwrite' a persistent U.K. deficit.

Suppose that all official holders of sterling were invited to exchange these obligations for interest-bearing obligations on a special IMF account (the interest burden would be borne by the U.K.). These obligations would be perfectly liquid and backed *in the first instance* (see below) by a group of countries in given proportions—say the members and proportions of the Paris Club. Thus if, for example, Ghana wished to reduce her IMF-sterling by £10 million, she would exchange it for a package of currencies— dollars, marks, francs, sterling, &c. These currencies she could, if she wished, exchange for other currencies or for gold. Whenever such a contingent claim on, say France, were exercised, a U.K. liability to France in gold would be established. However, the payment of such liabilities (i.e. U.K. to France, in this instance) would be staggered: settlements would take place over a period of time. New sterling balances would in other words be created at this point which would be both gold guaranteed and funded. If one of the club members liquidated any of her IMF-sterling holdings she would have an immediate claim on the U.K. for gold to the amount represented by her own 'backing' of the obligations; as regards the package of other currencies the position would be identical to that of a non-club member.

The meaning of an arrangement like this would be that in so far as sterling balances were secularly run down— say by newly independent countries in the course of development—the U.K. would have to bear the full cost in terms of a transfer of real resources. But she would be given time to pay: the club members would as it were 'back her bills' and accept delayed payment in exchange for a gold guarantee.

What about the reverse case—the running up of sterling

and dollar balances? Initially these might be held constant, but, to use the old nationalized-industry formula, 'taking one year with another'. One might stipulate that over the three years following the setting up of the arrangement the liabilities were not to rise net, but within the period, temporary increases would be possible. If the U.K. or the U.S. ran deficits that implied an increase of sterling and dollar liabilities over the period they would be forced to settle in gold or to try to persuade individual countries to hold old-style sterling or dollar liabilities: this would not always be easy.

There would thus be plenty of constraint on the U.S. and the U.K. not to run deficits: indeed many would consider a scheme such as this too deflationary. The merit of the scheme is that it would provide the key-currency countries with time and with rather more freedom to devalue without upsetting the international-payments mechanism. There would be no escaping their responsibilities, but there would be formal institutional guarantees that they would only have to meet them gradually.

Secondly, the European countries would be introduced in a minor way to the business of running reserve currencies. Thirdly, the way would be open to the development of a true international currency. Moderate increases in U.S. and U.K. liabilities could be agreed upon. As and when holdings of francs, marks, &c., increased, they too could be exchanged for IMF obligations. And as and when the IMF obligations were more and more firmly recognized as currency in their own right, they could be joined by the creation by the IMF of obligations based ultimately on not any one currency, redeemable by a package of currencies each of which could be converted into gold.

H

Linking aid to liquidity

A very attractive variant on the Triffin type of plan to turn the IMF into a super central bank has already been referred to in passing—the 'Stamp plan' devised by Mr Maxwell Stamp. The essence of this is to link aid-giving and liquidity-creating. New liquidity is created in the form of certificates credited to the reserves of under-developed countries and the industrialized countries agree to accept these certificates as fully transferable and part of their reserves. I doubt whether in fact a solution along these lines is likely in the near future to be acceptable on a scale which would make a major contribution to the problem of liquidity in general or sterling in particular. However it might, while providing a marginal contribution towards solving these problems, make a major contribution in the separate but more important field of aid for underdeveloped countries. A group of donor countries outside the IMF—the Development Assistance Group of the OECD is an obvious body—might well agree that as part of their aid programmes (and enabling these programmes to be somewhat larger than they would otherwise be) they would issue a limited number of aid certificates which could be spent in any country in the group and would be accepted by all the countries and counted as a part of their reserves. The EEC countries fear that this kind of plan is simply devised in the U.K. interest (see p.101). However, it is hard to see why bargaining among the donor countries should not result in a distribution of aid certificates among recipient countries in such a way that the donor countries are likely to share equitably the real burden involved in the aid scheme. The main merit of the scheme is that it might provide a way of facilitating the transfer of resources from any potential donor with underemployed capacity to underdeveloped recipients.

As such it deserves to be considered along with schemes for tying or untying aid, and generally for concerted aid policies.

However, it is probably a delusion that the two birds of liquidity shortage and aid shortage can be hit by the one stone. They are separate problems, and too great an expectation of the use of some kind of 'Stamp Plan' in a liquidity-creating context may lead merely to disappointment and frustration in regard to aid.

Further developments

While this section was in draft in the late summer of 1963, further developments in the field of international liquidity were rapidly taking place. The Americans moved still farther away from the almost total reliance on short-term bilateral arrangements which had characterized their policies in 1962. The re-thinking, which I have suggested was forced on them by the U.K.'s failure to join the Common Market, showed more plainly with every month. Mr Roosa's article in the *Business Review of the Federal Reserve Bank of Philadelphia*, published at the time of the 1962 meeting of the IMF, has already been discussed (p. 89). Just as the world's central bankers were preparing to meet again in September 1963 he published another article (in *Foreign Affairs*). As was widely noted, this was very different in tone. Though certainly not propounding any radical or concrete proposals for reforming existing institutions, it echoed President Kennedy's willingness expressed in July to consider the possibility of the need for reform. It was a decidedly 'multilateralist' document, compared with its predecessor.

In August the Federal Reserve Bank of New York published in its *Monthly Review* an article called 'Conversations on International Finance' written jointly by members of the

New York Federal Reserve Bank, the Banque Nationale
Suisse, the Banca d'Italia, and the Deutsche Bundesbank.
This was in itself a notable act of international monetary
co-operation and contains much useful discussion. It is,
however, an entirely 'bilateral' document—with not a hint
that there might be any case for any thoroughgoing multilateral reforms. Perhaps the most interesting section is that
devoted to the U.S. attempts to develop medium-term
'swaps' by the device of issuing special certificates and
bonds of twelve or fifteen months' life. The authors are
'inclined to recommend further careful exploration of the
potentialities of such special certificates and bonds which
might conceivably grow into a second line of defence
behind the swap network'.

At the IMF meeting the climate of opinion appeared to
be significantly different from a year earlier. Some people
were prepared to say that they thought the 'Maudling
Plan' had been dismissed too lightly at the previous meeting; and there was tangible evidence of a change in mood
in the setting up of two study groups to explore what
problems may arise in international-liquidity arrangements in the future and what methods might be appropriate to cope with them. One is an IMF staff group, the
other an extremely high-powered committee, drawn from
ten major countries (the members of the 'Paris Club') with
Mr Roosa as Chairman. These groups are to report their
findings to the annual meeting of the IMF in Tokyo in
1964.

It would be wrong, however, to make too much of any
shift in sentiment which has occurred. A number of the
Continental countries, particularly the French, made it
clear that they were still deeply suspicious of an Anglo-
American interest in liquidity arrangements and that they
still regarded the U.S. deficit as the main problem. The
deficit itself fell very sharply in the third quarter, perhaps

largely as a result of the measures adumbrated by President Kennedy in the summer, but at the time of writing it is impossible to say whether this is the beginning of a large and basic improvement.

Finally, we should note the publication of *The United States Balance of Payments in 1968*, a study prepared by the Brookings Institution. This expressed the view that the basic deficit seemed likely to have been eliminated by 1968 but urged that if this happened important new liquidity measures would be required. They argue strongly for a reformed IMF and the replacement of the key-currency system by an international reserve currency created by the IMF or a similar body. As a second-best alternative, if such a scheme is not acceptable to the world's politicians and bankers, they suggest a modified system of flexible exchange rates consisting of a sterling-dollar bloc and an EEC bloc. Within each bloc rates would be fixed but the rate between them could fluctuate.

The study is powerfully documented and argued but does not appear to have had much effect on the authorities in the major countries, at least so far.

8

Conclusions

AT the heart of all questions about currencies, exchange rates, and the balance of payments, lie issues of sovereignty. The plain fact is that economically, just as politically or militarily, the U.K. has not been sovereign since the war. This was brought home abruptly in the Suez adventure, but for most of the time it is something we have tended to blink at or forget. Only slowly, after a long process of double-think, are we coming to recognize the nonsense of an independent U.K. deterrent, and the necessity of relating our defence policy to a supranational framework. Not until recently have the government begun to accept the fact that politically we can no longer expect our independent voice to carry major influence in the councils of the world; many people still refuse to see that this is so. Failure to see or accept our lack of sovereignty in economic policy had led to many misunderstandings and bad policies. Many (though perhaps not all) of the fears of those who opposed Britain's entry to the Common Market on the grounds that we should no longer be masters in our own house were, therefore, beside the point. The formal surrenders of power to Brussels (such as they would have been) should have been viewed in the light of the existing *de facto* lack of power on the one hand, and the uses to which having a voice in Brussels could have been put on the other. However, that is all water under the bridge now. In principle, if not in practice we are alone in the world. How can we cope with the problems of managing our balance of payments and our currency?

One method of coping with the fact that our problems and commitments are too great for our unaided powers is simply to opt out of the problems and throw off the commitments: to cut ourselves down to size, as one might put it, to illuminate the psychological motives at work. Thus it was an overstatement to say in the previous paragraph that there was *no* nationalist alternative open to the U.K. In economic, as in political and military, policy there is a left-wing or radical nationalism: Mr Kaldor is to sterling what CND is to the bomb. This attitude seems to me misguided. The problems we refuse to deal with have to be tackled by somebody else, now or later. In an overwhelming economic catastrophe, such as occurred in the early thirties, no doubt our primary obligation is to save our own skins at whatever cost—though even in such situations, since everyone else is playing the same game the results are apt to be unsatisfactory. In the absence of a catastrophe, it makes more sense to try to work within the existing international framework in attempting to improve our position. What needs to be done?

We can distinguish three kinds of problems in the management of sterling. First, how to improve our long-term, underlying balance of payments; secondly, how to cope best with the fluctuations in the balance of payments which will inevitably occur; thirdly, what should be done about sterling as a reserve currency? The three problems are interrelated. The better the underlying balance the smaller the fluctuations are likely to be and the easier it is to cope even with bigger ones. According as one *defines* the underlying balance, so the fluctuations in it will differ. The fact of running a reserve currency exacerbates the fluctuations in the balance, rules out certain policies of adjustment, and perhaps makes the improvement of the underlying balance more difficult. However, although the problems are interrelated they are separable: no change in international currency arrangements is likely by itself to transform our balance of payments.

Before we can discuss policies for improving the underlying or basic balance we have to be agreed on what constitutes this. I have argued that what is normally taken (the balance on current and long-term capital transactions) is not the most appropriate balance, largely because many items within it are as volatile as some of those outside it (various kinds of privately held short-term capital). I have suggested a 'market' balance—which includes all unofficial transactions together with 'non-compensatory' official transactions—as better representing what we have to improve. The market balance has in fact fared considerably better than the 'current and long-term capital' balance in recent years.

This question of the volatility of particular items in the balance of payments has more general significance. I believe that insufficient attention has been given, in discussion and implementation of balance-of-payments policies, to the degree to which the expected effects of a particular policy will be permanent. Many policies will in fact, even if they act as expected, do no more than buy the authorities some time; but these policies are often represented as curative. In particular, much of the argument about improving the balance by working on the pressure of demand has been, in my view, beside the point. Of course, it may often be helpful, or even essential to buy some time until more fundamental correctives begin to work; and in the 1950s it was much more difficult to rely on international monetary co-operation for a breathing space than it is likely to be in the 1960s. On the other hand, it is crucially important to know exactly what one is doing; and too much has been made of our special difficulties. The plain fact is that our policies have not been good. There is no doubt that there has been a harmful 'election cycle'. The authorities were culpably slow in recognizing the existence and nature of cost-inflation and the appropriate cure for it. Possibly they concentrated too much on the niceties of short-term Keynesian stabilization policy before they fully realized the complexities of the situation they were attacking and the measures they were using; and did not concentrate enough on longer-term objectives for which errors in estimating the various magnitudes are perhaps less crucial.

As far as policies for permanently improving the balance are concerned, we are, I think, well on the way towards implementing some of the most important. We are probably nearer to achieving a workable incomes policy than any of our competitors. In many industries and in Whitehall much re-examination of existing practices and development of new ones has been going on. We know much more about the economy and about the timing and nature of the effects of particular measures; and we have added to the armoury of weapons at our disposal.

I have little to add to the suggestions for improving the balance of payments put forward in the NEDC reports; but there are two general principles which seem to me worth emphasizing. First, no system of accounts can reveal any of the causal relationships at work: it is dangerous to assume that if you can increase or decrease any particular item you will improve the balance correspondingly—the other items are unlikely to remain unaffected. Secondly (a partial corollary of the first principle) it will usually be better to aim at improving the whole economy—in terms of costs, efficiency, dynamism or what you will—than at working on improving the balance-of-payments sector in particular.

The conclusion reached on devaluation was that though

there are circumstances in which altering the exchange rate would be the best policy for the balance of payments, if sterling were not a reserve currency, it is not a genuine policy alternative so long as sterling *is* a reserve currency. This is where our lack of economic sovereignty is most striking. Obviously we have, on this ground alone, the strongest interest in the development of a truly international reserve currency—which would restore to us a genuine freedom to devalue—or, short of that, of the fullest international monetary co-operation to support the rate when it is in trouble. Further, it is in the light of our present lack of sovereignty that policies on exchange control should be framed. The extra vulnerability that results from relaxing exchange controls must be seen in relation both to our present vulnerability and to the development of international co-operation to reduce this. In so far as exchange liberalization is some kind of *quid pro quo* for co-operation (as it might have been had we joined the Common Market) there may be something to be said for it. However, one may be sceptical about how much foreign exchange is likely to be earned as a result of further liberalization; and such moves should certainly not be undertaken for prestige reasons.

Finally, there is the question of whether the U.K. should aim at replacing the key-currency system with one based on an international currency; or whether she should be content with a development of the existing system, bringing other countries gradually to share (in indirect ways) the burdens of running a reserve currency. There should be no doctrinaire answer. This is an area of means, not ends; and what is possible will depend largely on the attitudes of the Europeans and the Americans. The latter were for long unwilling to consider any radical multilateral system—perhaps because they were counting on a solution to the problem of sterling through the U.K.'s membership of the Common Market. Recently their attitudes have changed a great deal and their basic common interest with the U.K. may be asserting itself. It is more difficult to detect a change in the Europeans. Their view remains that any multilateral credit-creating scheme, in whatever form, will simply be a device for getting them to finance U.K. and U.S. deficits. It is wrong (though common and easy to do in this country) to dismiss their arguments too lightly. International credit creation is not a technical but a political matter; and we cannot have it until we have an international consensus to abdicate an important element of national sovereignty. I hope and believe it will come; but it will take time. On the other hand, however negative the Europeans may sound when they speak, they have shown repeatedly by their actions that they are prepared to support the dollar and sterling—both in crises and, less dramatically, over the long haul.

Much is happening and much more is likely to happen in the future. As long as the U.K. runs her policies reasonably (this does not mean deflation) she is likely to get, over the next few years, the short-run support she needs to tide her over difficult patches either formally from the IMF, or less formally from central banks. Meanwhile she should continue to press wherever it seems most fruitful, for further and more rational international arrangements. Since the main objection to a reserve system based on the IMF is to the discretionary credit-creating powers, it might be worth trying to set up first a non-creating IMF system which would constitute a half-way house. I have outlined one possible such system (rather analogous to the EPU) which would internationalize reserves but would involve the creditor countries in no more than institutionalized (as opposed to the present informal) short-term lending to countries in deficit. When some scheme such as this had been working for a while (and if perhaps there had also been some change in international creditor-debtor positions), it might prove easier to move to a completely multilateral currency.